LAURENCE OLIVIER

The author is the most distinguished English-speaking actor of the twentieth century. He has had a glittering sixty-year career in roles ranging from romantic Hollywood successes in the golden period of the 1930s, in *Wuthering Heights* and *Rebecca*, to towering and unsurpassable interpretations of classic Shakespearean parts, including Hamlet and Othello. As a film-maker, his revolutionary innovations in motion picture technique have brought Shakespeare alive for countless people in the films of *Hamlet*, *Henry V* and *Richard III*. As a director and producer whose stewardship of the National Theatre renewed a great tradition, he also introduced some of the greatest modern masterpieces, from O'Neill to Shepard, into the English repertoire.

CONFESSIONS OF AN ACTOR, Laurence Olivier's autobiography, is also published by Sceptre Books.

Lord Olivier lives in London.

Praise for CONFESSIONS OF AN ACTOR

'ON ACTING is a technical master class of considerable fascination and curiosity'
The Sunday Times

'The confiding quality is both maddening and endear-
ing. His egoism is charmingly unabashed'
Daily Telegraph

'This is not a modest book, and thank God for it . . .
solid theatrical truths, refreshing antidotes to some of
today's solemn introspection'
The London Standard

'Olivier is charming and disarming'
Books and Bookmen

'Here is the work of a perpetual student who wished
from the first to understand how a theatre breathes
. . . The book must be read in detail'
The Birmingham Post

Praise for CONFESSIONS OF AN ACTOR

'Actors and producers ought to contribute more to written history; they can often write quite as well as most journalists, as Olivier's book testifies'

The Listener

'A marvellous read . . . It is not, as one might perhaps have expected, yet another actor's discreetly told saga . . . Instead, with typical impetuosity he has chosen to tell all. It will undoubtedly be a bestseller, and with good cause'

Publishing News

'Lord Olivier, a great comic actor as well as a great tragedian, has produced some wonderfully funny anecdotes . . . wryly comic stories against himself abound . . . A remarkable book . . . a little of Larry on the night is more exciting than half a dozen actors' monologues'

Daily Telegraph

'Lord Olivier knows how to begin an autobiography . . . a genuine gift . . . CONFESSIONS OF AN ACTOR doesn't belong with, say, the Lana Turner–Lauren Bacall–Henry Fonda stories. Once again, Lord Olivier is in another ball park'

The New York Times

Laurence Olivier

ON ACTING

First published in Great Britain in
1986 by George Weidenfeld and
Nicolson Ltd.

Sceptre edition 1987

Sceptre is an imprint of Hodder and
Stoughton Paperbacks, a division of
Hodder and Stoughton Ltd.

British Library C.I.P.

Olivier, Laurence Olivier, *Baron*
   On Acting.
   1. Acting
   I. Title
   792.028'0924   PN2065

   ISBN 0-340-41238-0

Printed and bound in Great Britain
for Hodder and Stoughton Paper-
backs, a division of Hodder and
Stoughton Ltd., Mill Road, Dunton
Green, Sevenoaks, Kent (Editorial
Office: 47 Bedford Square, London,
WC1B 3DP) by Richard Clay Ltd.,
Bungay, Suffolk. Photoset by
Rowland Phototypesetting Ltd.,
Bury St Edmunds, Suffolk.

To my loved ones:
Joan, Richard, Tamsin, Julie-Kate

I would like to thank Gawn Grainger for editing the text of this book, and my secretary Shirley Luke for all her invaluable help.

L.O.

CONTENTS

PROLOGUE

Four years ago I wrote my autobiography, *Confessions of an Actor*. I thought then that I'd said everything that needed to be said about myself. I wanted to write my own book, as there seemed to be so many on the market about me by other people that I felt it was about time I put the real facts of my life down on paper as truthfully as I could express them, without the added trimmings of the sensational. Once it was finished, I felt that I'd got rid of a huge chore, the weight that had been sitting on me for two years was suddenly lifted and I was free once again. I was no longer chained to that monster machine that sat in the study and waited for my fingers and brain every morning.

Writing is not a glamorous occupation, as anyone who has attempted it will know; it requires hard work and self-discipline. It is lonely, it can be depressing; it creates an unwelcome feeling of vulnerability. I have heard writers complain of this before, but it always sounded somewhat exaggerated, 'Poor me, surrounded by my solitude.' Well, now I can tell you there is not a jot of exaggeration in it; it is the stark truth. Writing *is* a lonely profession, it is not romantic, it is a hard grind, a daily grind, and anyone who succeeds in filling up a page is a hero. It's rather like the man who kept banging his head against the wall and, when asked why he did so, replied, 'It's so lovely when I stop.' That's how I felt when I finished *Confessions*.

So why, four years afterwards, instead of looking at the beautiful Sussex countryside and listening to the mid-afternoon lark in between smiles and dozes, did I think of burying my nose in blank pages again?

It was those Sunday evenings that did it. Sitting round the

fire, chatting late into the night. The how, why, when chats –
you know the ones I mean:

'What was it like when . . . ?'

'How did you find that character?'

'Why did you play it that way?'

Not the usual boring theatrical gossip – he's sleeping with
her, she's sleeping with him stuff – but discussing in detail this
wonderful business of ours from the right angle. Searching for
origins, discussing beliefs, trying to explain what it was like for
me to be up there inside the Shakespearean greats.

The more I talked, the more I became fascinated by the way
it all came about. Of course it's always fun to talk about yourself.
I don't think anyone can deny that. I realized enough had been
written about me and my life, although very little had been said
on how it had happened, on what had been going on inside me
when I tackled some of the great roles. Slowly I put pen to
paper.

Any writer will tell you that the most depressing thing in the
world to experience is that early morning trudge to the dreaded
typewriter, sitting down and then staring at the blank page of
A4. There it is, this whiter than white piece of paper glaring
back at you from the roller, daring you to disfigure it with filthy
black type or only just legible handwriting. The brightness of
the white begins to affect your eyes. You sit down, you stand
up, you look the other way, hoping that when you turn again
some miracle will have been performed and the page will be full.
You walk, you talk to yourself, you ask how you ever got
yourself into this position in the first place. I'm an actor – why
have I given myself this chore?

The obstacles the writer puts in front of himself before he
finally gets to the study are more than in the Grand National
itself. There are papers to be read, letters to be relished, bills
to be paid, cheques to be signed. There are people to say hallo
to, instructions to be given; the day must be set in order. There
are agents to be phoned, gardens to be seen, and decisions
about what you would like for lunch. Where are my glasses,
where are my pens and pencils? I need my diary, I made some
notes last night.

How the hell did Shakespeare do it? Do you think he went through the same beastly process, or did it just happen for him? Did he have a direct line to the muse? I would answer without hesitation, yes. No matter what, I don't think he would have been wrestling over a blank page for too long; otherwise half of the plays would never have appeared. He must have been writing at a great pace, almost non-stop it would seem. It flowed. Tradition has it that he wrote continuously, poem, act, great scene. To the rest of us mortals that does not seem fair . . . but then no apportionment of genius seems that.

Perhaps Edgar Wallace had the easiest method of working. He would write a book in a day without putting pen to paper. He merely dictated everything into a dictaphone, then off to the races. No fool, Wallace. He would be placing his bets while the rest of us would only be into the second paragraph.

Thinking of Edgar Wallace gave me an idea. Why shouldn't I use a tape recorder? Direct speech would give my words much greater impact. They would be fresh and clear, spontaneous and immediate in a way I could never hope to achieve on the page.

At first talking into a tape recorder seemed easy. Soon it became a bore and even lonelier than writing. I sat there reminiscing into a lifeless machine day after day. What I needed, I soon realized, was an audience. Someone to react to my memories, stimulating me to conjure up the past. I found the perfect foil in Gawn Grainger, who very kindly spent a great deal of time listening to me and who was the editor of this book, for all of which I am most grateful.

This is not a book for the gossips; it is purely and simply about acting and about how I feel it has come about for me. Luck and more luck. The right decisions, even more fortunately the right opportunities for changes of style and at the right time. It is hard for me to know to which I owe the most: the apparent gifts, or the timing of my chances to exploit them. No matter what else I may or may not be, I am assuredly the luckiest man I know.

PART ONE

BEFORE THE CURTAIN

ONE

BEGINNINGS

Where do we start when we talk about the history of acting? Surely we have always acted; it is an instinct that is inherent in all of us. Some of us are better at it than others, but we all do it. The child plays games. The child cries when tears are the order of the day, endears itself to avoid criticism, and smiles when necessary; he predicts what reactions we require. Look behind those eyes that are giving the recipient the laughter that he expects, and you will see the veil of the actor. We have all done it at some time or another, and many of us still do – politicians, playboys, cardinals and kings. We wear the robes that we have designed for ourselves, and then act out other people's fantasies. This is singular; this is the monologue; this is the one-man show.

I think that in the beginning group acting was bound up with religion. That was the original theatre: dances to the gods for rain, for fertility; prayers and chanting, performing. You can still see it in parts of the world now, as it was. And in other parts of the world it is still there, but cloaked in subtlety.

Religious ritual was dominated by men. Women were left very much in the background. In fact, until comparatively recently, as we know, women were not allowed to appear on our stages. If we go back to the Greeks, women were not even allowed into the Olympic theatre, strictly taboo. There is a sweet story I heard somewhere; apparently one of the reasons for not allowing the women in was that the men had to be naked in order to be absolutely free. The story goes that there was a young girl, a newly married girl, who was madly in love with her husband. In order to be near him, she dressed up as a young man to get into the theatre. When her husband appeared and was successful in his performance, she rushed up to him and embraced him. Everything, naturally, came to a standstill. He said to her, 'You fool, they will kill you for this.' But so touched were they that they did not put her to death, which was the usual punishment. I am sure she lived to a ripe old age and told tales of her feat to her great-grandchildren.

One of the things that intrigues me about the Greeks is that they might have been naked in the theatre. They were naked for running, and I believe that they stripped to act in order to create an illusion of fitness, of speed, to streamline themselves rather like an Olympic swimmer of today – the smooth head parting the water. They shaved the hair on their bodies because it was considered unattractive. I have always done this myself if the part called for a show of legs. Maybe the nakedness was not for athleticism, but purely for absolute freedom. I wonder what it would be like to perform completely naked? That really would be the test, wouldn't it? Nothing to cover you apart from your imagination. If it worked, I wonder what the audience would really see. The Greeks must have gone beyond that, beyond the naked man, way beyond. I have done it in front of a mirror – I suppose we all have at some time – and I have seen what I wanted to see beyond the nakedness, the emperor's clothes in reality. Imagination working on top of imagination, both audience and actor in one. Fascinating. But this again is singular: the mirror and the man.

I thought that acting must have begun as a colloquy between two people – first of all, just two – which was later followed by single acts, by recitations, bards and all that. Somebody thought up the idea and for years I believed it came from the actors. I used to say, 'Don't tell me actors didn't come before writers.' Then I discovered, to my horror, that Thespis wasn't an actor, he was a producer. It was he who had the idea of two actors having a colloquy. It was *his* idea. I still can't believe it, but it's true. He was a producer, not an actor. He simply said, 'Let's have a conversation; you say this and you say that . . .' Maddening, infuriating. Thespian doesn't mean that to me.

On the other hand, I think he merely recalled his childhood. And if he did that, then I think we can safely say that the actor came first. Let's play mothers and fathers, doctors and nurses, cowboys and Indians. 'You say this and I'll say that.' Yes, I think it started long before Thespis. All that Thespis did was point a finger at conversation and remind us of things that had gone before. He took the improvisation and turned it into a play. He gave the players parts.

We can go back to the very beginning of time and we will find that the actor comes first. The games people play are developed and moulded until they eventually become the mirror for society to look at itself. We ape, we mimic, we mock. We act. The majority of people put acting behind them when they reach puberty and very often long before. But some of us who manage to leap the barrier of self-consciousness spend the rest of our lives acting out the dreams of others. Nothing comes easily, and I don't think it should. The child finds it easy, but then a child has a supple body and an open mind: fearless until taught fear; eyes wide, innocent and aware. That is something we should never lose, but sadly we do. The child becomes daunted by the shadows of the future; then the child becomes the adult; then the adult becomes aware of his mortality. Shakespeare knew this, and so should the actor. The actor should be able to create the universe in the palm of his hand. I often think that, if we could creep behind the eyes of the actor, we would find an attic of forgotten toys and a copy of the Domesday Book.

The complete actor, if there is such a being, would have all this plus a row of telephone operators seated behind his forehead, waiting to plug in to the next selection. A good actor is working in at least three levels at a time: lines, thought and awareness of the audience. A great actor has this and more.

He is able to plug into any one of his operators at the flick of an eyelid. He is always waiting to pounce at the slightest opportunity, wanting to get at the audience's jugular. A lion, a tiger, a leopard – there is something feline about him. But then

perhaps he is more subtle than that, more capable of disguise –
a serpent. That's it, a serpent.

Kenneth Tynan once said of me that I use my talent and
neglect my genius. Well, I don't think there is any room for
genius in the theatre. I think genius is too unreal a thing. You
can apply the word to other forms of art, but theatre is primarily
to do with practicability; in other words, there is no room for
genius. If a performance has a sudden flash of genius, where do
you start? Do you keep the members of the audience waiting
patiently till Act IV, Scene V of *King Lear* and then hit them with
one flash of genius and say, 'That's all I can do today'? I don't
think so. I don't think they get their money's worth like that.
Apart from anything else, I think they'd be deeply asleep by
then, or boosting the bar profits. On the other hand, if you're
practised, rehearsed and thoroughly versed, you've got something to offer. You know what the lines are about, but you
haven't waited for the final, ultimate way of saying them or
handling a single moment. Those things are still in the process
of being tried out and, with any luck, one or two will happen.
But you don't go on stage deciding to be a genius or saying,
'I'm not going to be a genius tonight.' You've got to produce
something; that's the job. You must present a mirror or an echo;
otherwise the audience will run screaming for their money back
or shower the stage with tomatoes. You take care of the play
and let the genius take care of itself.

Members of the audience must be respected; they must never
be underestimated. It's very easy to sneer behind your pocket
handkerchief and wink at your fellows in the wings, but among
that sea of faces beyond the footlights some will know. It is the
same wherever you go, in all forms of entertainment: you
respect them, they may respect you. They can be manipulated,
of course, but that's something else. This they enjoy, this is
why they are here, but they must not be handled clumsily or
obviously.

I learned about audiences at a very early age. You had to if
you wanted to keep the grown-ups awake on sleepy afternoons.

My sister shelters with cherished love a large wooden packing
case that was my first stage when I was about six. She still

keeps it in the trunk room. It is about the size of the inside of a car, and I used to draw curtains in front of it. My father always bought Gold Flake cigarettes in fifties, in circular little tins, and I would cut them up and put a candle in each so that I'd have little footlights. And there, in my theatre, I'd perform my own plays, entirely my own 'works'.

Let's pretend, as I have already said, is the original impulse of acting. I didn't know about Thespis, and I'm certain nobody told me. But there it was, in a wooden box, lit by candles in cigarette tins: the first Olivier Theatre. Of course, it becomes more difficult as the years move on. Acting really is a young enthusiasm, a childish excitement, a glamour that soon disappears. It is then that the hard work begins. The effort to improve yourself, to carve yourself into different shapes, to be successful, to be famous. What's the alternative? An office block and a bowler hat. In my case it might have been the Church. Mind you, that's not a bad auditorium.

The actor creates his own universe, then peoples it – a giant puppet master. The trick is to make the audience feel that they are observing reality, and this isn't easy, because to convey the word that has been placed in your mouth to a great number of people you have to exaggerate subtly, ever so slightly highlight. Lead the audience by the nose to the thought.

I hear remarks in the street or in a shop and I retain them. You must constantly observe: a walk, a limp, a run; how a head inclines to one side when listening; the twitch of an eyebrow; the hand that picks the nose when it thinks that nobody is looking; the moustache puller; the eyes that never look at you; the nose that sniffs long after the cold has gone.

Rhythms. Observe the speech patterns; keep them in your head, in your magic box. Store them until you need them, then use them. The way people walk down a bus or a subway train, one arm bent behind or both hands brought forward, elbows in as if in fear of accidental indecent contact. Then, in speech, the curious differences in lingual and dental contact. A weak R, the lisp that is just detectable. The plum that has somehow got itself lodged behind the epiglottis. The tongue that is too large for the mouth. The loose tooth, the false tooth. The adenoids that should have been removed in early years. The tight underpants that might raise vocal delivery somewhere towards the roof. The humble, the ingratiating, the toad. The jester, the minister, the king.

Try travelling on the London Circle Line underground. I worked on it as a gateman during the General Strike of 1926. It is exactly what it says it is: a continuous circle round London starting at A and returning to A. It is a favourite haunt for tramps in the winter, warm and snug, moving yet always returning to base. Get on, let's say, at King's Cross, and spend an hour returning to King's Cross, and observe. You will see more characters than you've ever dreamed of. It's quite astonishing. Go once in the early morning rush hour and then again in the leisurely afternoon. Everything you need will be there.

I sometimes look at faces and attempt to place them in another period; some lend themselves enormously to this, and others not a jot. The modern man, he's impossible. You can't dislodge him at all. He is never older than the second that has just passed. But period man, he's much more fun. You can re-costume him in your imagination and place him wherever you will.

I like to think that my face has always been an open canvas, ready to be moulded as I wished. It has always been my great joy to surprise an audience. Catch them on the hop. 'My God, is *that him*?'

Galleries are another place where lessons can be learnt. The National Portrait Gallery is a favourite place of mine. Here you can almost grow into the paintings. You can see how to shape a make-up by reading the highlights of the artist. Even in the Tate Gallery there is a lot to be learnt from Gauguin, Van Gogh, Turner. If you're in Amsterdam, look at Rembrandt's *Jeremiah Lamenting the Destruction of Jerusalem* – there is Shakespeare's Lear. Well, a part of him.

The zoo: some actors swear by it, and spend hours watching the animals. I agree this can help too, as witness my Othello, but to me the cages get in the way. What we are looking at, observing, is captivity: the lion or the tiger padding backwards and forwards, and dreaming of its native land. Captivity breeds its own particular movement, and I think the only way to learn from animals would be to watch them in their natural environment. Of course, observation in the zoo would work well if you were playing a prisoner, but there aren't too many of those parts around.

I once heard a story of a young actor who went to London Zoo when he was about to play the part of the Fool in *Lear*. He was standing in front of the baboons, when he became aware of someone behind him. He turned and recognized an older actor. The older actor looked at him for a moment and then pointed at the enclosure. 'When I played it,' he said, 'I was the one up in the corner with the red bottom.'

But when we talk of using animals as models, we are going back to the dawn of drama, to dance and to rituals. To the time when we performed as animals and donned animal skins. They were very much part of our make-up (not the Leichner kind): the bear, the lion, the tiger, the elephant, the ape. We mimicked them leaping about under the moon or the sun. We sacrificed them, we hunted them, and always we lived beside them. They might turn on us, we might turn on them, whichever became hungry first. We are always an inch away from death.

So we had our drama, and played out games, and performed before the king. We bent over backwards to entertain the elders. We tumbled before the tribe and told tales, stood on our heads and juggled with beads. We beat drums and blew notes through horns, we swung on ropes and walked through fires. And, above all, we danced, we beat out a rhythm with our bare feet on the warm earth. We worshipped the sun and the moon, and we performed rituals to make the corn grow and the rain fall. The actor was the centre of the village's attention. Even then he wore the two masks, the mouth rising in smile or drooping in sorrow. He could make you laugh or cry, sometimes both at the same time. He was the mirror of his time, the newspaper, the radio. If you stood in front of him, he could show you yourself. If he performed well he was applauded and given accolades in the form of garlands and trinkets; if he performed badly he was jeered and cast out – no different from today.

Well, there we were, drumming up our one-man shows, when along came Thespis. 'Thespian' is too flattering and broad a term

with which to describe the craft that we practise. I don't feel
that cheapness is all that cruel a jeer to be thrown at the initial
urge to do as we do; an 'interpretative craft' is all that is allowed
us by stern judgment; 'artist' must be a rarely justified boast for
us.

The actor has always been among us from the moment that
time began, and he always will be. And so it has gone through
the generations, the actor's inherent instinct to survive. We still
feel that at any moment the laughter will stop and the tomatoes
will begin. I don't think there has ever been any true actor who
has not felt this. To this day I still feel it and know I will go on
feeling it until I have given my final performance.

We actors stand by our present performance, not by our past.
We are as immediate as the moment. We give you our feelings
and hope that you will return yours. We ask for acceptance; we
are your servants.

Scratch an actor and underneath you will find another actor.

TWO

LESSONS FROM THE PAST

Burbage, Garrick, Kean, Irving: four names that handed on the Shakespearean mantle to our generation. That's why, today, performing Shakespeare, we can feel close to him; that his ink is still wet on the paper. Burbage did not know Garrick, Garrick did not know Kean and Kean did not know Irving, but it is the little cogs in between that make it all work, make it fascinating. Burbage created Hamlet and then, some time after, rehearsed a young actor, Joseph Taylor, in the part. Taylor played for the King's Company at the Globe and Blackfriars theatres. Being the second Hamlet and taught by the first, he must have automatically retained some of Burbage's original performance. Thomas Betterton played Hamlet and he studied with Sir William D'Avenant, who had seen Taylor. Garrick studied and learned from some of the older members of Betterton's company, and Kean from the survivors of Garrick's company, and then on to Irving. It all sounds very romantic, but looked at in this way it doesn't make William seem so very far away . . .

Clearly Richard Burbage, the first Shakespearean actor, must have been good, for he was Shakespeare's favourite. No matter how well liked you are by an author, if he does not think you are doing justice to his script, he won't use you.

Of course, one of the things to remember is that Shakespeare didn't know how marvellous he was. I wonder if Burbage did? Shakespeare had left Stratford and come to London. He got a job as a minor actor at the Globe playhouse, south of the

Thames. The company soon found that he was invaluable to them. He'd say, 'Look, I've had an idea . . . I've got an idea about that scene.' Then he'd give them three or four sheets of paper which would turn out to be magical stuff. After a while they would say to him, 'Look, Will, we need – oh, a good ten lines here. See if you can make the situation – you know what the situation is – just – can you sort of put a cap on it with that?' And Shakespeare would have this fantastic gift of doing so.

When I say that he didn't know how talented he was, I think that would only apply to the early days. By the time he was into his own stuff, I think he must have been very much aware. He was inspired in the realms of philosophy and philology: in almost everything he was fantastically marvellous. I think it was an Elizabethan – I was going to say fashion – but it was an Elizabethan gift, the use of language. If there hadn't been a Shakespeare or a Bacon, God knows what the English language would have been like, or would be like now.

So Burbage was the interpreter and must have been aware of what he was about.

What was he like, this man Burbage? What was he really like? Was he good or did he just happen to be around at the time, in the right place? No, he must have been good. William wouldn't have settled for rubbish. How extraordinary it must have been creating those parts for the first time. Hamlet, Lear, Othello. Did he know that four hundred years later actors would still be grappling with them? Were the two of them aware of the legacy they were handing on, or were they modern men only concerned with their time?

It is obviously difficult to visualize what Burbage was really like, but here is a description that I came upon by Richard Flecknoe, which would seem to give Burbage a seat on the throne of Thespis:

Burbage was a delightful Proteus, so wholly transforming himself into his part, and putting off himself with his clothes, as he never (not so much as in the Tyring-House) Assum'd himself again until the play was done; there being as much difference between him and one of our common actors as between a Ballad singer who only mouths it and an excellent singer, who knows all his Graces, and can artfully vary and modulate his Voice, even to know how much breath he is to give every syllable. He had all the parts of an excellent orator (animating his words with speaking, and with Speech and Action) his Auditors being never more delighted than when he spoke, nor more sorry than when he held his peace; yet even then he was an excellent actor still, never falling in his part, when he had done speaking; but with his looks and gesture, maintaining it still unto the height, he imaging age *quod agis*, only spoke to him: so as those who called him a player do him wrong, with only this difference from other mens, that is what is but a play to them, is his Business; so their business is but a play to him. (*A Short Discourse on the English Stage*, 1664)

Burbage's epitaph reads:

> *Hee's gone and with him what a world are dead,*
> *Which he reuiud, to be reuiued soe.*
> *No more young Hamlet, ould Heironymoe.*
> *King Leer, the greued Moore, and more beside,*
> *That lived in him, have now forever dy'de.*

Well, fortunately, they did not die; they were handed on. As I've explained, Burbage had schooled Joseph Taylor, who had been observed and remembered by Sir William D'Avenant, who in turn tutored Betterton, whose company passed it on to Garrick over a hundred years after the death of the first Hamlet.

It would appear that when David Garrick burst upon the scene, the theatre had been lulled to sleep by sweet tones: beautiful voices, lyricism, romantic, hollow, sweet cadences signifying little. Garrick arrived on the scene and things began to change. No longer the sameness of tone, now there were sudden starts and ominous pauses – dare we say a hint of reality? Here's an extract from Garrick's contemporary biographer, Thomas Davies, describing his début in London:

On the 19th of October 1741, David Garrick acted *Richard III* for the first time, at the playhouse in Goodman's Fields. So many idle persons under the title of gentlemen acting for their diversion, had exposed their incapacity at that theatre, and had so often disappointed the audiences, that no very large company was brought together to see the new performer. However, several of his own acquaintances, many of them persons of good judgement, were assembled at the usual hour; though we may well believe, that the greater part of the audience were stimulated by curiosity to see the event, than invited by any hopes of rational entertainment.

An actor, who, in the first display of his talents, undertakes a principal character, has generally, amongst other difficulties, the prejudices of the audience to struggle with, in favour of an established performer. Here indeed they were not insurmountable; Cibber, who had been much admired in Richard, had left the stage. Quin was a popular player, but his manner of heaving up his words, and his laboured action, prevented his being a favourite Richard.

Mr Garrick's easy and familiar, yet forcible style of speaking and acting, at first threw the critics into some hesitation concerning the novelty as well as the propriety of his manner. They had been long accustomed to an elevation of the voice, with a sudden mechanical depression of its tones, calculated to excite admiration, and to intrap applause. To the just modulation of the words, and concurring expression of the features from the genuine workings of nature, they had been strangers, at least for some time. But after he had gone through a variety of scenes, in which he gave evident proofs of consummate art, and perfect knowledge of character, their doubts were turned into surprise and astonishment, from which they relieved themselves in loud and reiterated applause. They were more especially charmed when the actor, after having thrown aside the hypocrite and politician, assumed the warrior and hero. When news was brought to Richard, that the Duke of Buckingham was taken, Garrick's look and action, when he pronounced the words, '– Off with his head! So much for Buckingham!' were so significant and important, from his visible enjoyment of the incident, that several loud shouts of approbation proclaimed the triumph of the actor and the satisfaction of the audience. The death of Richard was accompanied with the loudest congratulations of applause. (*Memoirs of the Life of Garrick with Anecdotes of Theatrical Contemporaries*, 1780)

The great theatrical volcano had erupted once again, and a giant was standing astride the London scene. Garrick was to rule until his death in 1779. He must have been very special indeed, towering above his contemporaries and blazing a theatrical path towards the next century.

There is in Mr Garrick's whole figure, movements and propriety of demeanour something with which I have met with rarely in the few Frenchmen I have seen and never, except in this instance, among the large number of Englishmen with whom I am acquainted. I mean in this context Frenchmen who have at least reached middle age; and, naturally, those moving in good society. For example, when he turns to someone with a bow, it is not merely that the head, the shoulders, the feet and arms, are engaged in this exercise, but that each member helps with great propriety to produce the demeanour most pleasing and appropriate to the occasion. When he steps on to the boards, even when not expressing fear, hope, suspicion, or any other passion, the eyes of all are immediately drawn to him alone, he moves to and fro among the other players like a man among marionettes. From this no one indeed, will recognise Mr Garrick's ease of manner, who has never remarked the demeanour of a well bred Frenchman, but this being the case, this hint would be the best description . . .

This is an excerpt from a letter by Georg Christoph Lichtenberg. He goes on to say:

. . . He has complete command over the muscles of his body. I am convinced that his thick-set form does much towards

producing this effect. His shapely legs become gradually
thinner from the powerful thighs downwards, until they
end in the neatest foot you can imagine; in the same way
his large arms taper into a little hand. How imposing the
effect of this must be you can well imagine. But this strength
is not merely illusory. He is really strong and amazingly
dexterous and nimble. (*Lichtenberg's Visits to England*,
1938)

Garrick sounds the complete actor. He must have been astonishing to observe: '. . . The eyes of all are immediately drawn to
him alone.' Does this mean that the other members of the
company were pretty dull? I don't think so. I imagine he was
supported by good actors, but that *he* was up there with the
gods.

Garrick took over the Theatre Royal, Drury Lane, in 1747,
just six years after his London début. He seems to have been
a good manager and caring about the members of his company.
He brought a discipline into the theatre that hadn't been there
before. Where things had grown shoddy and slapdash, he
insisted on neatness and concentration. Actors had long since
made up their own versions of the author's original, a sort of
bastard version of improvisation. Garrick changed all this. He'd
drop an actor, rather like a player in a football team, until he had
learnt to respect the audience and the author. What had happened was that actors had become lazy and probably, after a
while, believed their versions of the text were the correct ones.
We have all done this at one time or another. What he eventually
achieved with his company was amazing ensemble playing. For
confirmation of this, here's an extract from Davies's memoirs
of the time:

. . . I need only mention one of the plays he revived; the
Every Man in his Humour, of Ben Jonson, where all the
personages were so exactly fitted to the look, voice, figure
and talents of the actor that no play which comprehends so
many distinct peculiarities of humour was ever perhaps so
completely acted; and to this care of the manager restoring

this obsolete play to the stage may very justly be attributed its great success.

It sounds as though Garrick achieved the complete playing that has been emulated since by such companies as the Berliner Ensemble, the Moscow Arts, the Dublin Abbey, the RSC, and, I like to think, my own National Theatre Company.

To achieve true theatre, you can't have one man up front and the acolytes with their backs to the audience feeding the great star with lines as dull as dishwater. What you must have is every character believing in himself and, therefore, contributing to the piece as a whole, placing and pushing the play in the right direction. The third spear carrier on the left should believe that the play is all about the third spear carrier on the left. I've always believed that. If the character is nameless, the actor should give himself a name. He should give himself a family, a background, a past. Where was he born, what did he have for breakfast? Perhaps he has troubles at home, perhaps his wife has left him, perhaps his wife has just presented him with a new baby, perhaps he is saving for something – and so on. If the actor brings on with him a true belief in himself, we should be able to look at him at any moment during the action and see a complete three-dimensional figure and not a cardboard cut-out. To transport an audience, they must see life and not paste.

The theatre lost its ensemble playing after Garrick and didn't find it again until the great companies of Irving. In between came Edmund Kean, who was born in 1787 and was definitely a one-man band.

Kean's greatest asset was his dedication – something all actors must have. They cannot just turn on and turn off whenever they fancy. They must have dedication and determination, blinkered and only concerned with the self that wants to get up there and act. They must be totally egocentric and prepared to climb, clamber, elbow, jostle and scythe their way through to the top. If, at the end, they still have friends, they are remarkable. Doesn't sound very attractive put like that, does it?

Edmund Kean had all of that and more, and he wore himself out by the time he was forty-four. What an extraordinary man he must have been, 'the Sun's Bright Child'. He walked from Birmingham to Bristol with his family in tow to gain employment; one of the children died on the road. He signed contracts, and unsigned contracts. He bulldozed his way through society – perhaps not a very likeable man, except to the group of syco-phants who drank with him in the Coalhole in the Strand. I imagine he must have been completely self-centred and, when not enjoying adulation, was out of his brains with alcohol. But, in spite of this, the pleasure he gave has lived on through the years. Perhaps I'm a little hard on him; I mean, after all, I didn't know him. He really must have been very special indeed. What was it Coleridge said of him; 'It's like reading Shakespeare by flashes of lightning'? He arrived on the scene and extinguished Kemble almost overnight. Hazlitt said of his Richard III:

> He gives animation, vigour and relief to the part, which we have never seen surpassed. In one who dares so much, there is little, indeed, to blame. The progress of wily adulation, of encroaching humility, was finely marked throughout by the action, voice and eye. He seemed like the first tempter to approach his prey, certain of the event and as if success had smoothed the way before him. Richard should woo not as a lover, but as an actor, to show his mental superiority and power, to make the others the playthings of his will. Mr Kean's attitude in leaning against the side of the stage before he comes forward in a scene, was one of the most graceful and striking we remember to have seen. (*A View of the English Stage*, 1818–21)

Before the booze got to him he must have been quite startling: the little wild man, eyes blazing and brain full of poetry. He must have been very physical, athletic and strong. I think he was a tumbler when he was a boy.

The story goes that on his first night at Drury Lane, an unknown playing Shylock, Kean was living on the south side of the River Thames and didn't have the money for the toll to cross the bridge. So he swam the Thames instead. I'm sure it's a huge exaggeration and probably didn't take place at all, but it's a lovely thought. He more than likely put the story about himself. There's nothing like a piece of romantic public relations. But even if he didn't do it I'm sure, if it had been necessary, he would have done. As, indeed, I would. Determination.

His first night at the Theatre Royal must have been quite extraordinary. He had not rehearsed with his fellow actors, which was the custom in those days. The moves were set and the star would come in. No doubt he had a dress rehearsal, but even that is not established. If he had, he probably just walked the role, so nobody would have been aware of what was about to happen. He was entirely new to the London scene. Of course, the management would have seen him, probably in Dorchester where he was very popular, and not just on the stage.

The Theatre Royal was looking for a new star. Everything was happening with the rivals at Covent Garden, but not at the Lane. It is said that on the first night the Theatre Royal was half full, probably half full with curiosity. News would have got about that an unknown was going to play Shylock. He must have been electric. In the interval, the thrilled audience from the Lane mingled with the audience from Covent Garden, and soon the word was about. By the end of the evening the Theatre Royal was packed and cheering – and Edmund Kean was a star.

I like to think there is some truth in the story. I'm sure there is. So far as Drury Lane was concerned, Kean was a gamble – but what a gamble. He paid off in capacity box offices. He took the theatre by the scruff of the neck and shook it back into life. He carried the Theatre Royal on his back and thrust it up into the big time again. He was a major star and a major classical actor.

Obviously we cannot believe everything that is written about him; no man is without bias, and none more so than critics. But somehow I feel there must be a lot of truth in what Coleridge and Hazlitt said. They were men who were respected in their time, and when you consider that Hazlitt went to see Kean play Richard no less than three times in 1814, twice in February and again in October, writing about it on each occasion, there must have been something worth watching. It is such a shame that the only records we have are on paper. There is a prompt copy

of Kean's *Richard III* in the British Museum, where the dear
little Assistant Stage Manager inserted the maestro's inflections.
From this we can get a vague idea of how he performed
rhythmically and where he paused, and what, perhaps, he may
have sounded like. But the rest, like Kean himself, has gone in
the flash of Coleridge's lightning.

So what did he pass on? I think his approach was probably
the nearest we have to the modern theatre of today. A reality.
I think he burst through the romantic form and presented a raw
freshness that knocked the audiences sideways, the audiences
that had held Kemble up as a god. I think he opened their eyes
to the truth and thrilled them out of the boxes.

Of course, in the early 1800s they were still happily booing
and hissing and throwing things – not always tomatoes. By the
end of his life Kean knew both sides of his audience's face. Leigh
Hunt said of him two years before his death:

> Now, Kean we never see without being moved, and moved
> too, in fifty ways by his sarcasm, his sweetness, his pathos,
> his exceeding grace, his gallant levity, his measureless dignity;
> for his little person absolutely becomes tall and rises to the
> height of moral grandeur in such characters as that of Othello.
> We have seen him with three or four persons round him, all
> taller than he, but himself so graceful, so tranquil, so superior,
> so nobly self-possessed in the midst, that the mind of the
> spectator rose above them by this means, and so gave him a
> moral stature that confounded itself with the personal. (*Tatler*,
> 1931)

There was, in addition, a generosity about Kean. When a
friend asked Kean to help him out by appearing in his benefit
performance in Liverpool, Edmund agreed with alacrity. He was
to play Richard III to his friend's Duke of Buckingham. They
repaired, naturally, to the local hostelry and talked about good
times, bad times and old times. By the time they got to the
theatre they were warm inside and in the head. After Edmund's
first speech the audience began to scream, 'Mr Kean, you're
drunk!' After a long pause, he stared with those penetrating

eyes at the hostile house and replied, 'If you think I'm drunk, wait till you see Buckingham.' This story has been told many times over the years and attached to other actors, but I believe it started in Liverpool around 1830.

I don't think Kean's mantle was picked up until Henry Irving came along; he was born five years after Kean died. Of course there were others in between. Irving didn't start acting at birth or, if he did, nothing is recorded. But I don't think they were in the same league. There was Charles, Kean's son, but he seemed to be suffering under his father's name, though he did make rather a good career for himself. Then, of course, there was Macready, but anyone who is remembered solely for their pause can't have been that hot. No, for me, the mantle came straight on to Irving.

Kean was Irving's idol, though, of course, he never saw him; but on the first night of *The Bells* he must have felt very close to him. Again, rather like Kean's Shylock, Irving's Mathias did not open to a full house. However, in no time at all it was the talk of the town and Irving had the English theatre in his hands. His determination must have been similar to his idol's. Once he was acclaimed, he became the master and champion of his profession.

Perhaps an example of Irving's determination and dedication is shown in the story of what happened on his way home after his triumph at the Lyceum on that first night, 25 November 1871. He turned to his wife, Florence, and said, 'Well, my dear, we too shall soon have our own carriage and pair.' After a pause, Florence apparently said something in the heat of the moment which she may have regretted the rest of her life: she said, 'Are you going to go on making a fool of yourself like this all of your life?' Irving told the driver of the brougham in which they were travelling to stop. I believe they were at Hyde Park Corner. Without saying anything, he got out and raised his hat, saying, 'Goodnight, my dear, we shall never meet again', and his wife completed the journey alone. He never returned home, and he never spoke to Florence again.

I think Irving and Kean must have approached roles in a similar fashion, because both searched for the truth, both had flashes of fire; but I imagine as human beings they were very different. Although the Coalhole tavern was closer to Irving's Lyceum than Kean's Theatre Royal, just a question of crossing the road, I don't think the tavern's clientèle would have seen much of the great man. Irving became a leader of his profession in every sense of the word, whereas Kean, when work was done, only too quickly returned to a world of oblivion – the Coalhole. Not that this affects either's contribution. What was shown in both men's spotlit world was uplifting, exciting and unforgettable, and, although they never met, Kean's hand touched Irving's through the voice of others. The five-year gap between a death and a birth was bridged by Kean's contemporaries who had decided not to creep into their wooden overcoats with the assistance of John Barleycorn as Kean had.

The one thing the two great actors certainly had in common, apart from their talent, was that they both died penniless. But, as Irving said, he had 'not been sent into this world to collect money'.

My generation was brought up on the memory of Irving. To me he was a great idol, though I didn't see him, being born two years after his death. The hand-touching continues. Actors mimicked him and then passed their mimicry on to us. We were young men doing our own thing, but we all loved to sniff the past in our nostrils. When I was a young actor, Irving was clearly remembered. There was still a romance about his last night on a stage: how he had altered Becket's line, 'God's will be done', to 'God is my judge'; and when he recited Becket's last line, 'Into thy hands, O Lord, into thy hands', he had fallen to the floor facing upstage, his head literally and symbolically towards the altar. (He would normally have fallen downstage towards the audience.) Probably only half truths, but nevertheless an anecdote romantic enough to transport the listener to the wings of the Theatre Royal, Bradford.

In my company of 1963, I searched for actors who were as capable of playing Richard, Othello or Lear as I was. I was determined to surround myself with good actors and first-rate directors. I didn't want any wimps who would disappear into the shadows or, indeed, go the other way and shine out like a spotlit sore thumb. I didn't want someone who, as Beverley Baxter once said of Ken Tynan when he was an actor, 'waves at his friends in the audience and exits through the scenery'. I wanted people who were prepared to outgun me, I wanted the new cream of the British theatre, and I think I got it. Looking back at my company and seeing what has happened to them over the years, establishing themselves as leading actors in their own right, I think I succeeded. It has always been a thrill and a joy for me to see a new talent emerge, grasp the bit between its teeth, and race down the course.

We should encourage and not stifle. I'm sure Garrick did this, and Davies's report confirms it. He surrounded himself with the best people of his day, and left the dross. Of course, there weren't as many actors around then as there are today but, because of that, I think there were probably more good ones than bad. I think the ones that were involved really wanted to do it. It wasn't a question of, 'Oh, well, if I fail my exams to become a doctor, I'll settle for acting.' It was much more than that. Of course, a great many people were born into it – the family trade, as it were.

I heard a lady once say to her son, 'But my dear, you surely don't mean you would become an *actor*!' – making it sound like Lady Bracknell's 'A handbag!' Even in my youth the actor was still on the fringe of society. He was to be patronized rather than accepted; he was an amusement, a plaything still looked upon as a rogue and a vagabond. Romantic, but not socially enticing, all right for placing a discreet hand beneath the mistress's skirts, but not conducive to walking up the aisle and sharing a golden band. Irving was the first individual actor to become socially acceptable, but even today there is an air about the profession which says 'wrong side of the sheets'. So, in Garrick's day I believe you were either born into it, or simply had to do it or die.

When Garrick took over Drury Lane, he was determined to make it the best playhouse in the land, and not just a crown in which to place his own theatrical jewel. He wanted the best and fought to get it. He was a great one for rehearsing, which had really been unheard of before, a play being put on in five days at the most. Garrick worked at them for weeks, and would cut, rewrite and add scenes if he felt it necessary. He would use the ideas of his company as well as his own, which was the start of true ensemble.

There is a story about the rehearsals of *Every Man in his Humour*. An actor in the company called Woodward, considered one of the best comedians of his day, appeared very attentive to Garrick's direction while rehearsing the part of Bobadil. However, during Garrick's absence one morning, he decided to do it his way and had the rest of the cast falling about and applauding his antics. During this exhibition Garrick came in at the back of the playhouse undetected and watched what was going on. After a time he came forward and let his presence be known, much to the embarrassment of Woodward. There was a stunned silence. All looked to the great man. He paused and stared back. The class had been chalking on the blackboard while the teacher was out of the room. He stepped up onto the stage and went over to Woodward. Another pause then, suddenly, 'Bravo Harry! Bravo! Upon my soul, bravo! Why, now, this is, no, no, I can't say this is quite my idea of the thing . . . yours is, after all . . . to be sure, rather . . . ha!' Another pause. Woodward, embarrassed, replied, 'Sir, I will act the part, if you desire it, exactly according to your notion of it.' Another pause, and a smile from Garrick: 'No, no, by no means, Harry. Damn it, you have actually clenched the matter. But why, my dear Harry, would you not communicate before?'

If we are to believe it, and I do, we can hear the actors still breathing in that company. The manager caught the moment and used it. Instead of creating an embarrassing scene or creeping away and pretending that it had never happened, he took Woodward's idea and saw what he could do with it. I'm sure, from that moment on, he had a staunch ally in Harry Woodward.

The same has happened to me on more than one occasion. My actors at the National seemed to have an uncanny knack of doing devilish impersonations of me. I believe there is still a tape around, though I have not heard it, of an imaginary conversation on Waterloo Bridge between myself, John Gielgud, Ralph

Richardson and Richard Burton, all done by the one actor, who, needless to say, has gone on to become an international star in his own right. I must do an impersonation of him one day.

When his production of *Every Man in his Humour* opened, Garrick was still only thirty-three, a young man in his prime. It was said of Woodward's performance, which had been encouraged by Garrick, that it was his masterpiece in low comedy.

Some thirteen years later in 1763, Garrick, by this time well established as actor and manager, decided to make changes in the theatre itself. He decided to rid the theatre of stage spectators. Until then there had been two audiences, one on the stage and one in the auditorium. Often there were so many on the stage that the actors had little more than a pocket handkerchief to work on.

It was often the case that when an actor had a benefit, he would arrange for his friends to be in the stage boxes, rather like a party. Consequently, there were some disastrous results. An actor called Holland was performing Hamlet for his own benefit and, on seeing the Ghost, reacted with such reality that his hat flew off. When Hamlet complained that the air 'bit shrewdly' and was very cold, a female friend of Holland's who was a stage spectator calmly got up, crossed the stage, picked up the hat and replaced it on Holland's head. The house erupted in peals of laughter and the Ghost, without any more ceremony, left the stage followed by a very embarrassed Mr Holland.

Problems also arose over exits and entrances. If the stage spectators were in force, it was often difficult to make one or the other. A certain actor playing Falstaff was apparently covered in so much padding that it took him a full five minutes to squeeze through. Very often the actor was greeted by his friends and held in conversation too. So Garrick decided to remove the stage spectators, but came up against a lot of opposition, as it would mean a decrease in revenue and would certainly affect the pockets of the actors on their benefit nights. He and his partner, James Lacy, eventually got round this by deciding to enlarge the theatre. Providing that the space before the curtain contained as many people as had formerly filled the pit, boxes, galleries and stage, there could be no complaints. The enlarge-ments were completed in 1762, and from that time onwards only the actors were allowed on the stage.

It then, of course, became the custom to entertain in the dressing rooms, and sometimes an interval could last as long as an hour and, if Royalty were backstage, even longer. But going to the theatre then really was a night out, according to Georg Lichtenberg:

Hamlet has folded his arms under his cloak and pulled his hat down over his eyes; it is a cold night and just twelve o'clock; the theatre is darkened, and the whole audience of thousands are as quiet, and their faces as motionless, as though they were painted on the walls of the theatre; even from the farthest end of the playhouse one could hear a pin drop. Suddenly, Hamlet moves towards the back of the stage slightly to the left, and turns his back on the audience. Horatio starts, and saying, 'Look, my Lord, it comes', points to the right where the Ghost has already appeared and stands motionless before anyone is aware of him. At these words Garrick turns sharply and, at the same moment, staggers back two or three paces with his knees giving way under him; his hat falls to the ground and both his arms, especially the left, are stretched out nearly to their full length, with the hands as high as his head, the right arm more bent, and the hands lower and the fingers apart; his mouth is open; thus he stands rooted to the spot, with legs apart, but no loss of dignity, supported by his friends, who are better acquainted with the apparition and fear lest he should collapse. His whole demeanour is so expressive of terror that it made my flesh creep even before he began to speak. The almost terror-struck silence of the audience, which preceded this appearance and filled one with a sense of insecurity, probably did much to enhance this effect. At last he speaks, not at the beginning, but at the end of a breath, with a trembling voice: 'Angels and ministers of grace defend us!' – words which supply anything this scene may lack and make it one of the greatest and most terrible that will ever be played on any stage. The Ghost beckons to him: I wish you could see him, with eyes fixed on the Ghost, though he is speaking to his companions, freeing himself from their restraining hands, as they warn him not to follow and hold him back. But at length, when they have tried his patience too far, he turns his face towards them, tears himself with great violence from their grasp and draws his sword on them with a swiftness that makes one shudder, saying: 'By Heaven! I'll make a ghost of him that lets me!' That is enough for them. Then he stands with his sword held out so as to make him keep his distance, and, at length when the spectator can no longer see the Ghost, he begins slowly to follow him, now standing still and then going on, with sword still upon guard, eyes fixed on the Ghost, hair disordered, and out of breath, until he, too, is lost to sight. You can well imagine what loud applause accompanies this exit. It begins as soon as the Ghost goes off the stage and lasts until Hamlet disappears . . .

I don't think I'd have approved of the applause at the end of the scene, but the rest sounds magnetic.

So there we have it. Burbage, Garrick, Kean and Irving. Great volcanoes as far as I am concerned; heads high above the rest of the field. I believe that these four were the true innovators. They came along when the theatre needed them and shook it into life again.

It would appear that I am dismissing the others in between, and I suppose I am, but that is not to say that they were not good. I'm sure some of them were very fine indeed – fellows like Betterton, Macklin, Quin, Phelps, Kemble and, of course, dear old 'pause' Macready – but for me it was the four who built the signposts.

However, there was one man later whom I did see and who certainly had an influence upon me. It was 1924; I was seventeen, alive, active and full of tomorrow. I spent a lot of my time in those days sitting in the galleries of London theatres, looking down at the fashionable talent of the day, drinking in, remembering, learning. At this time a man came to London, a man who was very special, very immediate and very different. He was from another planet as far as my young eyes were concerned. I decided that for this man the gallery must be put aside; I needed to be in there, floor level, where I could see the eyes. I spent the extra and stood in the pit. Through the whole house there was a feeling of expectation. Whenever I walk into a theatre I feel that I am at home, and that night it was even more so. I was tingling, nerve-ends excited, eyes open, waiting. The last bar bell went, the last empty seats were occupied, the front of house lights dimmed, the chattering stopped and there was an expectant silence. A pause, a beat, then the curtain went up:

> *Who's there?*
> *Nay, answer me, stand and unfold yourself.*
> *Long live the King! . . .*

Everyone waiting for Scene II.

> *Let's do it, I pray; and I this morning know*
> *Where we shall find him most convenient.*
> *[Exeunt.]*

> SCENE II
> *Though yet of Hamlet . . .*

On, on . . .

> *A little more than kin and less than kind.*

There he was, the amazing Jack Barrymore, on stage at the Haymarket. Everything about him was exciting. He was athletic, he had charisma and, to my young mind, he played the part to perfection. Although American, his English was perfect. He was astounding. He had everything going for him, including startling good looks.

My Hamlets in later years owed a great deal to Jack Barrymore. It seemed to me that he breathed life into the character, which, since Irving, had been lulled into arias and false inflections, all very beautiful and poetic, but castrated. Barrymore put the balls back. I'm not saying he was next in line after Irving, I don't think he was or perhaps I did not see enough of him, but

I think the 'old boys' would have approved of his approach. When he was on stage, the sun came out. Some critics knocked him for his verse speaking as, indeed, was to happen to me in later years. They were wrong, I know they were wrong. He had a way of choosing a word and then exploding it in a moment of passion. Perhaps you did not always agree with the choice, but it was constantly riveting. He would vary pace, but never gabble, always understandable. There would be a sudden burst and then again a lull, rather like the wind freshening up before a squall. For my money he really seemed to understand Hamlet.

Barrymore was the top man in the American theatre, a colossal talent, perhaps a little too leeched on by Hollywood, but then that was a temptation that affected all our generation for a time. I'm sure that if Beverly Hills had been around for Burbage, Garrick, Kean and Irving, they would have found themselves on a fast boat to the New World before breakfast.

It would seem to me that Barrymore was the direct link with Edwin Booth, 'the Prince of Players', probably the first of the great American actors. Booth's father, Junius Brutus Booth, was a contemporary of Kean, so it's easy to see how things slowly match up, like a detective story. The hand stretching down from Burbage finally crossed the Atlantic.

Not only were Kean and Junius Brutus Booth contemporaries, they also performed together, alternating the roles of Iago and Othello, both in Britain and in America. It is said that Kean used to upstage Booth by eating grapes and digging the pips from between his teeth with his dagger during Booth's big speeches. Possibly true, but I'm sure Mr Booth must have added a few touches of his own.

Perhaps I have quoted too much in this chapter, but I wanted you to be able to see through the eyes that were there. The past is one thing, but it is in the present that we live, and it is in the present that we perform.

We can learn from the past and, of course, so we should. We must retain and reject, but we mustn't forget the present.

Do we get wiser as we get older, or have we just, like an old dog, learnt a few extra tricks? I am seventeen going on eighty. I have learnt, I have discovered, I have dismissed. I have led,

I have been led, nose-ringed by the past. In the end we must decide for ourselves, but it is making the right decisions that counts, deciding and holding on to your own beliefs, for it is you, and only you at the end of the day, who can look after yourself. No one else really cares; you don't need glasses to see that self-preservation is on the menu. You must have the strength, the will and the determination of an ox, and you must believe in your own beliefs. Can a man preach from a Sunday pulpit and not believe? I think not, for if he does we will surely see the dust on his dogcollar. We must, in the end, look to ourselves. We can take counsel, we can take advice, but in the end *we* must decide, it must be *our* decision. This is not to say we mustn't learn – we must. We must pick the brains of those who went before us; watch, learn and listen, research and discover, but, above all, the final decision must be our own.

Moments will remain in our memory, things that we have thought valuable, stored away somewhere in those decaying memory cells. Of course, there will always be a flavour of the past, for the past is a fact, but it is the future we should be looking towards, because it is the future that will be looking back at us. It is the future that will be looking at yesterday, which is our present, and in its turn will decide whether to retain or reject. This does not mean that we should perform with one eye on posterity, but that we should perform with integrity. Youth will always impersonate until it has found its confidence and its own roots.

I am seventeen going on eighty. I will continue to learn until all ceases to function. I know that the earth turns and that the sun sets and the sun rises, but I must always remember that somewhere in the shadows there are new things to be seen.

Blazing away out there are the spirits of Burbage, Garrick, Kean and Irving, lighting the theatrical sky for ever. Smiling, grinning, laughing and saying, 'Follow that!' I think that's how it always will be: 'Who's on next?' It's the music hall with the act numbers lighting up at the side. It's not important to be top of the bill; it's important to be the best.

Not everyone can join those giants straddling the theatrical world, grinning down at the Lilliputians, but we can try. We must try. Above all we must be good. That is all we can be, good. It is for other people to daub the statue with what they will: genius, greatness, or whatever. But for this brief moment we are here, treading the mill that has been trod before, getting our ankles wet and hoping that the horn will not be too green for too long. Lead me by the nose, Richard, David, Edmund, Henry; lead me by the nose and then release me. Let me make the judges think that I am the best bull in the ring.

New actors, new waves, new ideas – it's all been done before. What we forget is that every new generation is the modern man. We are only watching things repeated with different costumes, new settings, original surrounds. However we look at it, it is still the same jewel shining from the crown that was mined between 1564 and 1617.

> *Good friend, for Jesus sake forbear*
> *To dig the dust inclosed here,*
> *Blest be the man that spares these stones,*
> *And cursed be he that moves my bones.*

I like to think that some of our writers of today will live, and somewhere in the next century they will be mounting new productions in the orbital stations in the sky. I am convinced that those great spinning metropolises of the future will have a theatre tucked into their bosoms somewhere. In the next century, instead of going on tour to Manchester, Nottingham, Birmingham, change trains at Crewe, it will be Orbital Station Two, followed by Orbital Station Three. I can see the shuttle from Heathrow now, blasting off the launching pad, arrowing into space with a troupe of National Theatre Players on board. Somewhere between here and Mars an essayist or, perhaps, a computer, will be discovering an actor for the first time: 'Last night on Station Three we saw the most exciting *Richard III* since . . .'

PART TWO

THE GREAT
SHAKESPEAREAN ROLES

THREE

HAMLET

I have lived with Shakespeare all my thinking life – the greatest dramatist of all time; to some the greatest poet, philosopher, man. With a flick of his pen, he can twist an audience from laughter to tears. His genius is unparalleled. He writes roles that any actor worth his salt would find the means to play by hook or by crook. He is matchless in wit, power, imagination, fire, philosophy . . . I could go on for ever. But what he has above all is a magical sense of theatre. His stories, though many of them are stolen and have been told before, are moulded and fashioned in such a way that they shine as though they have been newly minted this morning. Whenever an actor comes to him, he should come with hunger and excitement. To make his language work from your brain to your fingertips is to fulfil your profession. You can come back to him time and time again, attacking the same role, and there will always be something new to discover. They say that even a bad actor playing Hamlet will get something right.

It has always been my intention to make Shakespeare as modern as possible. I don't mean in production, I mean to the ear. In my early days I was attacked for this – 'Can't speak the verse' – but I was arrogant and confident enough to ride this criticism, and I think I have been proven right. When *Henry V* happened, the audience knew what I was talking about. They weren't listening to someone singing an aria; they were hearing a man's thoughts set before them as clearly as I could. On the first night of *Hamlet* at the Old Vic, Tyrone Guthrie, my director, came to the dressing room and said about my make-up, 'Every inch a Hamlet. Think they'll probably fault you for the verse speaking and, to a certain extent they may be right, but you will come to your own decisions about that in your own good time, I expect.' I had to decide whether to rethink and obey the critics, or battle on and hope the critics might come to me.

An example is a production John Gielgud and I did of *Romeo and Juliet*. It's very easy, looking back, to criticize, but in those days there was a way of doing things. That's how they were *done*, and that's what the public came to see. They wanted their verse spoken beautifully, and if that was not how you delivered it, you were considered an upstart, an outsider. So I was the outsider and John was the jewel; and a shining one too, deservedly so. John still has the most beautiful voice, but I felt in those days he allowed it to dominate his performances and, if he was lost but for a moment, he would dive straight back into its honey.

I thought his first Hamlet was wonderful, because he didn't allow himself to do that, he didn't sing. But as time went by I believe he sang it more and more. His fifth or sixth performance of Hamlet, as far as I was concerned, was a complete aria. For me this was a great disappointment. I said to myself, 'That's wonderful in its way, but has he not gone backwards?'

Of course his voice was musical enough to sell it to the people on the old grounds. He was giving the familiar tradition fresh life, whereas I was completely disregarding the old in favour of something new. Somehow I feel that he was a little led by the nose by his audience and by his acolytes. He was greatly admired, in fact adored, and like all of us at some time in our careers he believed his publicity. So, by the time we did *Romeo*, I was considered by the Establishment to be against him. Everybody was in his favour, while I was on another planet. I can still remember some of the awful headlines. You always do, don't you? The good ones dance through your head and are forgotten in a day; the bad ones become indelibly stamped forever. Here's one from the *Evening News*: 'A beautiful Juliet but . . .'

What the hell! I think I was right, and I know that John will go on thinking that he was. Whatever the results, whatever side people come down on, we must have been fascinating to watch.

I wonder if he'd agree with me now? My outsider theories that were so against the Establishment of the time! They must have thought I was pretty mad in those days, but on the other hand they can't have thought I was all that bad, for they went on employing me and the public continued to watch.

When I did my *Hamlet*, I wanted to project this man's thoughts to people who had never had the opportunity to hear them before. Of course Shakespeare can be read, and indeed is – witness our schooldays. Reading him is better than nothing, but for my money his plays have to be seen. Presented by an actor, interpreted and projected from the other side of the curtain, that is where my job lies, that is the nature of my particular beast. You may not agree with my interpretation, but it is up to me to sell it to you as best I can.

Theatre is more than a collection of effects, exits and entrances. The actor must take the audience on a journey; with tragedy, because the journey is predictable, the end must be cathartic. When you know what is going to happen, the point is twice as strong. It is a double realization. (This is also true of comedy. The second time you do the same gag, it brings the house down.) Rhythm and timing are needed to create effects which must also appear to be spontaneous: it is the seeming absolute spontaneity of reaction which makes the audience feel a moment of recognition, of new understanding. Reading may be better than nothing, but it is not the same as feeling and understanding Shakespeare's great lines through the interpretation of an actor.

Shakespeare was originally a popular playwright, a people's playwright, but as time and language changed so did our theatrical intelligence. We stopped listening. Perhaps the actor stopped making us listen. We have only to go back to Kean to find the theatre full from pit to gallery with a cross-section of society. They ate oranges in the stalls, and nobody had heard of matinée teas. Socialites may have waved from box to box, but not when Mr Kean was on stage.

Somewhere in the wasteland of my early days Shakespeare
had got lost or had been vocally abused out of all recognition. I
hope now that he is back on the topmost pedestal where he
truly belongs. He has been mutilated, mugged and masticated.
He has been taken to the heights by some of our greatest actors,
and to the depths by others. He has been translated, truncated,
humiliated and musicalized. He has been quoted, quartered and
pulverized; butchered, bullied and bashed beyond all recognition;
misquoted and mismanaged; played by men, women and children
whenever the fancy took them. He has challenged us all and
won hands down. He has made fools of most of us at one time
or another. There he stands, finger on cheek, quizzical, slightly
bewildered, but passing the baton through century after century.

My God, I wish I'd met him, talked to him – but above all,
heard and listened.

Hamlet, in my opinion, is pound for pound the greatest
play ever written. It towers above everything else in dramatic
literature. It gives us great climaxes, shadows and shades; yet
contains occasional moments of high comedy. Every time you
read a line it can be a new discovery. You can play it and play it
as many times as the opportunity occurs and still not get to the
bottom of its box of wonders. It can trick you round false corners
and into cul-de-sacs, or take you by the seat of your pants and
hurl you across the stars. It can give you moments of unknown
joy, or cast you into the depths of despair. Once you have played
it, it will devour you and obsess you for the rest of your life. It
has me. I think each day about it. I'll never play him again, of
course, but by God I wish I could.

The first time I was to play the part, at the Old Vic, I felt it
was crucial to establish that Hamlet was bone real from the very
first word. I was determined to take the audience with me, to
make them believe that this man lived. I knew that earlier
players of this part had thought that Hamlet should begin on a
strange note, but I decided it would be kindest to my audience
to keep it simple, not to frighten them to death with the high
theatricality of my opening.

Whenever an actor first attempts Hamlet, he should be aware
that it's a sporadic collection of self-dramatizations in which he

tries to play always the hero and, in truth, he feels ill cast in the part. His imagination is working as though he is a hero, but his soul is working in the brave light of the author, who decided to write a play with a hero who wasn't a hero. Witness the soliloquy 'How all occasions . . .' following hard upon his staring enviously at Fortinbras, the ideal man of the times.

Many years ago, when I was first to play Hamlet at the Old Vic, I went with Tyrone Guthrie, who was going to direct it, and Peggy Ashcroft, who was going to play Ophelia (but for some regrettable reason wasn't able to), to see Professor Ernest Jones, the great psychiatrist, who had made an exhaustive study of Hamlet from his own professional point of view, and was wonderfully enlightening. His book on the subject was called *What Happens in Hamlet*.

We talked and talked. He believed that Hamlet was a prime sufferer from the Oedipus complex. There are many signals along the line to show his inner involvement with his mother: one of them is his over-devotion to his father. Nobody's that fond of his father unless he feels guilty about his mother, however subconscious that guilt may be. Hamlet's worship of his father is manufactured, assumed, he needs it to cover up his subconscious guilt. The Oedipus complex may, indeed, be responsible for a formidable share of all that is wrong with Hamlet. I myself am only too happy to allow to be added, to Shakespeare's other acknowledged gifts, an intuitive under-standing of psychology. Why not? He was the world's greatest man.

At one moment Professor Jones said, when he was talking about primitive painters' ideas of various occurrences, that there was a painting that was of particular psychopathic interest. It was *The Conception of the Blessed Virgin Mary*, which shows an angel blowing the pollen from a lily into her ear. He said, 'Of course, the ear hole is also the sign of vicious tendencies, possibly of a homosexual nature, you know.'

In amazement I asked, 'The *ear* hole?'

'Yes,' he said, waited a minute, and then – very quietly (not for Peggy's ears) – 'any orifice but the right one.' I thought this was very funny and could never get it out of my mind when I was playing Hamlet; the pollen going into the ear, blown by an angel from a lily.

I can't remember if Jones came to see the production; I don't think he did. But I warned him that he would not find the Oedipus theories overt, though, of course, they would be there. He said, 'I wouldn't suggest you should make it overt, as long as you know about it. That's the important point. You're not supposed to tell the audience with every wink and nod that part of the reason for your present predicament is that you still wish you were hanging on your mother's tits.' A very entertaining man.

Talking about finding new meanings in the text, it for ever being fresh, I thought of one the other day. In the grave scene when Laertes is mourning Ophelia and the unknown figure announces, 'This is I, Hamlet the Dane', I believe he is saying, 'I am King' – echoes of his father, whom he must have heard saying this in anger at some time or another, maybe on a number of occasions. When I was playing it, I just thought that the outburst was merely another show of temperament, another side of his self-expression. But no, he had to find other people to be all the time, and it didn't occur to me that at this moment it was his father. The audience wouldn't have known for a second what I was at, but it would have helped me greatly. There can be found a slight hint of it, but a sweetly tender one, during the duel with Laertes, when his mother drinks the poison obviously intended for Hamlet.

Hamlet's continuous complaining throughout the play is expressed directly to the audience, and he says almost in as many words no less than twice, 'It's no good, I can't do it, can I? I wish I knew why. Am I a coward? Who dares pluck my beard? Am I this? Am I that? It's no good, I can't.' Many people read into that the first pacifist; indeed, some remark that he's the first hero that any author dared create out of a hero who was no hero at all. But there are others, and I think this makes a marvellously firm argument for his Oedipus complex, who say he can kill his uncle/father when he is behind the arras, because he can say to himself he didn't know it was him . . . alas, poor Polonius. It is *after it is done* that he shouts victoriously to his mother, 'Is it the King?' in the desperate hope he has done it without knowing it. He would rather act a part than do it: rather stab through a curtain than stab the king.

When Laertes has knifed him and death is a few breaths away, he is suddenly free to wreak vengeance because he has the innocent, pure reason of vengeance for himself, not for his guilt over his mother. Once he realizes he is about to touch hands with death, he is free, his guilt is expunged by his own murder, and he is able to feel, 'You murder me and I'll murder you.' For me that makes a final keystone in the arch of the argument for the Oedipus complex.

Though I believe this theory, I do not believe it to the extent of letting the play be just about that. The play is about a character who has that particular eccentricity, that particular thing *in* his character. When one thinks of audience after audience for nearly five hundred years trying to work it out, it is fascinating. Shakespeare was simply pouring out all that was in his instinctive heart at the time: it is an extraordinary exploration into the human mind.

'The man in black' is always interesting; as an actor your job is to enable the audience to follow his journey from one characteristic to another, from mood to mood. The actor must be absolutely clear in his mind where is going, whatever theories he has nursed (and over the years there have been many); in the end he must tell the story.

But the questions keep on coming up, and always will. Was Hamlet this? Was he that? Did he do this, did he do that? *Did he sleep with Ophelia?* In reply to this last, one old actor manager, early in the century, said, 'In *my* company, *always*!' As far as I'm concerned there was nothing platonic in the relationship: when it's played as brother and sister I have no time for it. Hamlet is not just imagining what is beneath Ophelia's skirts, he has found out for himself – country matters – for certain. 'Get thee to a nunnery, why would'st thou be a breeder of sinners?' Ophelia's problem is that she truly believes that the four-poster will become permanent and legal, and that she will eventually wear the crown of Denmark. Hamlet's problem is that he wants to follow his mother to the bedchamber as well . . . and does? Most unlikely – but the Gertrude/Hamlet scene in the first production I did at the Old Vic went about as far in this direction as I dared suggest, or the Ghost's complaints would have been on a different score.

I had always decided that if I ever had the chance to lead a company I would start off with the big one, and in 1937 the chance came and I did. Of course, I was still not forgiven by a lot of the critics for my verse speaking, and there were still odious comparisons, as I suppose there always have to be. It may be the young actor today has to suffer because my shadow has been left upon certain roles; not that I'm objecting now, you understand. In those days Gielgud was the top dog when it came to verse speaking and his Hamlet was very popular, with me as with the majority of theatregoers.

I was determined to win through and, in the end, I think I did. But perhaps that's not for me to say. Truth . . . speak the truth, though the verse will not entirely take care of itself. Shakespeare knew what he was doing; he put the rhythms there and he didn't wish them to be ignored.

Looking back now, forty-eight years later, it is difficult to see that performance with absolute clarity, though there is still a warmth that remains with me. People who have never experienced that walk between one wing and another will probably wonder what I mean by warmth. It gets in the nostrils and in the hair, it is a combination of electric light, glue, rancid paint and scent. It is like a favourite teddy bear, or getting off an aeroplane into the warm sun. Once experienced, it stays for ever, calling the actor back again and again, like a siren's song.

Memory is one thing, but action is for the immediate man. I still feel immediate. Every morning when I wake I think, to hell with the doctors, the temperature-takers, the people who tamper with you like a pre-war pressure cooker, telling you to sit in your wicker chair in high summer and muse. I should be out there where I belong, on the planks of wood that we call 'the boards'. I should be out there holding the old enemy at bay and trying to persuade them to believe it, to see it my way. I should be soaring away with my head tilted slightly towards the gods, feeding on the caviare of Shakespeare. Eyes telling all, and each member of the 'congregation' thinking that I am talking to them personally. I was made to perform, and it is not easy to be put out to grass, left to feed on memories and friendships. An actor must act.

Whatever people may have thought of my Hamlet, I think it was not bad. I know it was not perfection, but it *was* mine. I did it. It was *mine*.

The film interpretation of Hamlet was also all mine. I still think, after all these years, that the film stands up, much cut though it had to be, and I am still proud of it. A film can never show you what the actor was really like on the stage, but it can give you a very clear idea and, as a medium, I have grown most wantonly partial to it. Its powers are apparently limitless.

Like any great play, *Hamlet* is totally adaptable. By this I mean it can be performed anywhere with anything. It can have a set, it can be played in drapes, it can be done before a brick wall. It lends itself to 'the corner of the room'. This was the directive Sir Denys Lasdun was faithful to in designing the theatre generously named after me, 'a large room with an audience embracing a corner of it'.

I think, probably, one of the best performances I was involved in was at Elsinore in Denmark. Pouring, drenching rain meant that we could not open outside as we had intended to and, consequently, after a hurried discussion, it was decided that we would perform in the ballroom, which meant a rapid re-staging. Tony (Tyrone) Guthrie, our director, was busy organizing things for the real opening, and something had to be arranged about seating for future performances, so he was heavily involved in administration. He left it to me to set it up and rehearse the new moves around the strange area that was now to accommodate us. As he went off, he said, 'Fix it for me, Larry. Just place it all as you think best.' So I did. All the movements had to be changed, so all the lovely invention was left to me. As you can imagine, I was thrilled to do it and, of course, enjoyed myself wildly.

There is nothing better than a group of actors being presented with a problem of this kind and having to improvise. When time is drifting away and the performance is getting closer, somehow the adrenalin creates an excitement that runs through everyone, from the leading actor/actress to the maker of the tea. Everyone pulls together with the one object in mind. It is at such times that you can ask for the impossible, and get it. 'I'm afraid the only way you can play this scene is by hanging from the chandelier, dear boy.' Without a moment's hesitation, the reply would come back, 'Of course – no problem.'

Great God! there is something amazing about them, the band of players. There is a comradeship that I've only experienced once elsewhere, but not so happily, in the Services.

Somehow every performance seems to be enhanced in times of unexpected difficulties; there is an edge, a fine edge that hoists the players, even the least inspired, on to another level. All the actors' motors have to be running, but in a low gear for greater acceleration. Nobody dare get a moment wrong. Whereas laziness, even boredom, may have crept in before – and this is very understandable when you think in terms of standing night after night on the end of a spear with somebody else delivering the dialogue that you feel you could do better – that boredom, for a moment, is forgotten and the contribution becomes genuine, energetic and electric. Everyone becomes a thoroughbred, muscles alive and alert. The vibes are high, and this will affect the audience as well. What they witness will be a night that they will always remember. 'Were you there that night at Elsinore? I was.' It is amazing how many people now think they were there. Rather like Harold Pinter's *The Birthday Party*, during its brief first run; if all the people who now claim they were there had, in fact, been there, it would have run for a year.

Whether what the audience sees is good or not, we will never know, but the energy that is directed towards them will engulf them. In Elsinore that night the actors were heroes, every man jack of them. I know – I was right in the middle of it. A dignity and excitement was achieved, an atmosphere in which no one falls on their arse unless it is intended. Everyone thrills with a sense of achievement and importance – and quite rightly. The 'one for all' society syndrome. Above all, the performance was spontaneous.

I remember giving the stage to Torin Thatcher at one moment; he was playing the Ghost. We had erected a little stage for the play scenes and stuff, with some stairs that led up to it. I knelt by the stairs, facing away from the audience and when, as the Ghost, he turned at the top, he found himself in this glorious solo upstage position. It was magnificent. I remember remarking to Tony Guthrie, 'Wasn't it heavenly when Torin found himself so placed for his big scene with me?', and Tony replied, 'Yes, it flowed through the ballroom like warm strawberry jam.' I took it as a compliment!

It is a great night to remember, full of magic and memories. Some say it was the best thing they'd ever seen. Whether it was or not I'll never know, but it must have been something special. It rained, and, because of this, the gods came over to our side. I think they always do, if handled with respect.

Enough has been said about Hamlet by others with better literary qualifications than mine; all I know is that he has a million hidden problems that you can never quite explain. He is utterly unlike Coriolanus, who is absolutely straightforward with no particular psychological interest. Coriolanus is himself, he knows it, his mother knows it. I can tell you how I crept inside him, inside Othello or Richard; but I cannot tell you how I crept inside Hamlet, the man. Hamlet just takes you by the hand and either treats you roughly or shows you the way to the stars. All I know is he captured me, and once he had, he never let me go.

Scholars have not stopped theorizing about *Hamlet* since the day that Burbage played its first performance. So what I feel about it, though important to me, is probably no more than a drop in the ocean so far as the academics are concerned, but it does have the special authority of the practitioner.

I suppose it must have been performed more times than any other play in the English language, with every performance at least slightly different, which is fascinating to think on. It is, without a doubt, the best play ever written, partly perhaps because it lends itself to so many changes and interpretations. The actor, however he plays it, good or bad, will get something right in his journey from the castle walls to his final silence.

I could see it and read it for ever. Yes, the best play in the world.

FOUR

HENRY V

In my first season at the Old Vic in 1937 I wanted to be completely different in every performance. This is nothing new to an actor, of course, indeed it is what every actor should be about, but I was determined to demonstrate as much versatility as possible. Something that has always been part of my theatrical life: I like to appear as the chameleon. Nothing has given me more pleasure than knowing I have tricked my audience and been on stage for more than five minutes without being recognized. As I have always said, I am a character actor, not the leading man who seeks applause on his first entrance. I want the joy of dressing up, not applause for a handsome profile. So all my career I've attempted to disguise myself, probably to no better effect than I did in the double bill of *Oedipus* and Mr Puff in Sheridan's *The Critic*. The joy of being an actor on that night was completely intoxicating. There are some occasions when you stand in the wings and cannot wait to get in front of the audience, and that was one of those moments. You can smell the excitement, feel the adrenalin pumping, like being drunk on spring water.

I have always looked for something new; that's what keeps the batteries recharged and the mind young, that's what keeps the cement from setting between the ears. I'm constantly looking, observing, storing the images away in my theatrical locker. A cough here, a blink there – all remembered, noted and put away in the mental drawer until needed, brought out, dusted and used. As Brecht said in one of his last poems, 'You can make a fresh start with your final breath.'

Thus it was that, when I joined the Old Vic in 1937, I was looking for a way that I could show off my versatility. Why not jump in at the deep end? First Hamlet; then Sir Toby Belch, a complete contrast; and finally Henry v. Not bad for a first season, I thought.

All went well, apart from the odd critic not approving my verse speaking, until it was time to get working on *Henry V*. Suddenly I panicked. I didn't think it was the play for me at that time. It seemed wrong, I was frightened of the heroism. England had completely changed in the 1930s: the whole atmosphere of the country, which was frequently mirrored in the theatre, was against heroics. Plays like *Journey's End*, which had been so successful in the 1920s, would not have survived for a week in the late 1930s. We had moved away from all that, heads stuck firmly in the sand, rooting for pleasure – herds of people searching for truffles. We were sophisticated and viewed the world from the end of a cigarette holder. Little did we realize how soon we would change. Shortly Germany would bare its teeth, and our generations would become just as heroic as the one that had gone to the trenches before.

It is strange looking back. It's rather like diving into a pool, but in reverse, the body coming out of the water feet first and returning to the top board, feet together, arms stretched forward.

Having thought a great deal about *Henry V* and still being very unsure, I spoke to my dear friend Ralph Richardson, who was always reliable with his advice as far as I was concerned. I trusted him and I think he trusted me.

'Henry the Fifth,' he muttered and thought for a moment; then his eyes twinkled. 'He's a scoutmaster.' He spoke in tones of disgust. He paused again, and then in those unforgettable tones of his he said, 'But he raises scoutmastership to godlike proportions, which Shakespeare always does.' Another pause. 'Of course you must play him.' So play him I did.

Rehearsals began and, still fearful, I started by completely undercutting Henry, something that I don't think I can often be accused of doing during the course of my career. I fought against the heroism by flattening and getting underneath the lines, no banner waving for me. 'God for Harry, England and Saint George' was not going to ring out across the footlights like a poor night at a third division *Gang Show*. I was being so natural at one point that I think my fellow actors must have had difficulty hearing me. The night scene really was a night scene, my fellow actors were going to have no difficulty sleeping, and I'm sure if I had played it this way the audience would have joined them.

One morning Tyrone Guthrie spoke. He had never given me a great deal of direction; until then he had left me alone, given me my head, and for this I was grateful. I remember with *Hamlet* he had let me go and simply backed me up right the way through to the first night and beyond. But, as I say, on this particular morning at rehearsals he spoke.

He was a tall man and his looks were a combination of Jonathan Miller and Charles de Gaulle – a very striking, dominating appearance. He had a habit of snapping his fingers when he wanted attention. I think that anybody who ever worked with him will remember them as the loudest finger snaps in Christendom. I swear that when they snapped at the Old Vic, they could be heard outside the theatre. Snap, they went, and the rehearsal came to a halt.

'Larry . . . Let's have it properly.'

'Properly?'

'Properly.'

'Tony, I am doing it properly.'

'Like this . . . this is how I want it.'

He went into 'This day is call'd the feast of Crispian . . .' and, as he built up towards the end, he vocally began to climb a ladder. Heroics, bloody heroics. I looked at him for a moment and saw that, if he had been wearing the right hat, he could have done a good impersonation of Baden-Powell. He stopped and looked at me.

'That's the way to do it.'

'Like that?'

'Like that.'

'Tony . . . ?'

'If you don't do it like that and enjoy doing it like that, you just won't carry the audience with you.'

He was right. I was fortunate to have him directing me and directing *for* me. I followed his eye. He knew.

So the Henry V which was to make me famous as an actor who could be heroic, and which I was later to film, began there at the precise moment when the fingers snapped and the 'scoutmaster' recited the lines rather badly; he was no actor, but he pointed me in the direction which I had fought against, and he was right.

I worked on the great arias, moulded and fashioned them to me, and then from Guthrie's launch pad, took off. I was heroic, nobody could have been more so, but I was truthful, I was not showing off; I played the man like a trumpet as clearly and truthfully as I knew how.

I'm not ashamed to say that I stole from people. I've never been ashamed of that. If something is good then take it, borrow it, as you will. When young actors copy my characterizations, I am flattered, as I'm sure Irving would have been of the generation who impersonated him. It is not arrogance, it is understanding.

As I have said, I admired Barrymore and used much of his Hamlet in mine. In the case of Henry V I have to acknowledge some of Lewis Waller's performance. I was fascinated by his vocal acrobatics and I'm certain some of them lingered on within me – honed to my performance, of course, but still there.

> *Once more unto the breach, dear friends, once more;*
> *Or close the wall up with our English dead!*

(Confident, encouraging, steady, lead them and prepare them.)

> *In peace there's nothing so becomes a man,*
> *As modest stillness and humility;*

(Hold them, let the words work.)

> *But when the blast of war blows in our ears,*
> *Then imitate the action of the tiger;*

(Begin to feel that tingle in the base of the stomach, prepare, get ready for a change of gear.)

> Stiffen the sinews, summon up the blood,
> Disguise fair nature with hard-favour'd rage;

(Stay in control but begin to feel the excitement. Then change the intonation.)

> Then lend the eye a terrible aspect,
> Let it pry through the portage of the head
> Like the brass cannon; let the brow o'erwhelm it,
> As fearfully as doth a galled rock
> O 'erhang and jutty his confounded base,

(Up a gear and beginning to move, the words blazing in front of you.)

> Swilled with the wild and wasteful ocean.

('Swilled')

> Now set the teeth and stretch the nostril wide;
> Hold hard the breath and bend up every spirit
> To his full height . . .

(Now we're really motoring, climbing vocally but in complete control. The politician and the hero.)

> . . . On, on, you noblest English!

(Patriotism)

> Whose blood is fet from fathers of war-proof;
> Fathers that, like so many Alexanders,

(Change the tune to as natural a one as is humanly possible.)

Have in these parts from morn till even fought,
And sheath'd their swords for lack of argument.
Dishonour not your mothers; now attest,
That those whom you call'd fathers did beget you.

(*Now take them with you, they want to come, climb the ladder.*)

Be copy now to men of grosser blood,
And teach them how to war . . .

(*Now, like any good politician, speak to them collectively in such a way that they think you are speaking to them individually.*)

. . . And you, good yeomen,
Whose limbs were made in England, show us here
The mettle of your pasture; let us swear
That you are worth your breeding; which I doubt not;

(*Got them . . . now hold them. Remember never give them everything.*)

For there is none of you so mean and base,
That hath not noble lustre in your eyes.
I see you stand like greyhounds in the slips,

(*Moving up the ladder, pace, excitement, almost flying.*)

Straining upon the start. The game's afoot:

(NOW LET GO.)

Follow your spirit, and upon this charge,
Cry . . .

(*We're there.*)

. . . 'God for Harry, England and Saint George!'

(*Take off .*)

When it worked it was an amazing feeling, being in complete control of body and mind, the whole machinery meshing perfectly. It was heroic all right, but that's what it needed; Tony Guthrie was right. Even the critics were beginning to listen to me on a new wavelength.

Within two years fighting began in earnest and the anti-heroic brigade went out of the window. When the war was under way I found myself on occasions going round military camps with a one-man turn that I had worked out. It was geared to whip up patriotism and was, I believe, very successful. It began with a poem on the death of General Havelock. Who the hell is he, I hear you say. Well, if you walk up Whitehall, turn and face Trafalgar Square, he's the one on the horse on the left-hand side. Sir Henry Havelock, a great hero in his time, having relieved the beleaguered British residency at Lucknow on 25 September 1857. He, along with Campbell and Outram, put down the Indian Mutiny. As Trevelyan says, he stamped the flame out in central India before it could spread. A year later the British Government had replaced the East India Company, and twenty years later Disraeli persuaded Queen Victoria to assume the title of Empress of India. For his deeds Havelock was cast in metal, placed upon a horse, and now resides in Trafalgar Square.

Anyway, I began with this poem, which was full of good old heroic stuff, and then went into

> *This day is call'd the feast of Crispian:*
> *He that outlives this day, and comes safe home,*
> *Will stand a tip-toe when this day is nam'd,*
> *And rouse him at the name of Crispian.*

By now I knew how to pace it all perfectly and was able slowly to whip up my wartime audience of real soldiers, urging them forward with me:

> *And hold their manhoods cheap, whiles any speaks,*
> *That fought with us upon Saint Crispin's day.*

During the applause I would hold my gesture and remain still. Then, when I felt the applause reach its peak and begin to wane, I would launch into 'Once more unto the breach . . .' By the time I got to 'God for Harry . . .' I think they would have followed me anywhere. Looking back, I don't think we could have won the war without 'Once more unto the breach . . .' somewhere in our soldiers' hearts.

When I made the film, I taught my horse to break into a gallop at a certain moment in the speech, somewhere about 'Be copy now to men of grosser blood,/and teach them how to war . . .' The horse seemed to know the lines as well as I did, and would prick up his ears and go every time I got to 'Saint George'. When the film was complete Arthur Rank, the producer, asked what I'd like by way of a bonus, and much to his surprise I asked for my horse, which he happily gave me. I kept him at Notley and rode him whenever I could. When this was not possible, for exercise we used to put him in the trap and take him to the station to meet guests, petrol being rationed at the time. I remember on one occasion going to meet Noël Coward who was coming for the weekend. I picked him up and there we were, ambling slowly home through the perfect English countryside.

'Doesn't go very fast,' clipped Noël.

'Want more speed, do you?' I asked.

'Yes,' replied Noël.

'Hang on a minute,' I said, and leaned over towards the horse's ears.

'Once more unto the breach . . .' I started, and sure enough by the time I got to 'Be copy now . . .' he went into a gallop, and galloped all the way home.

So there you are: the part I fought against fought for me. Henry took me by the hand and hurled me into the theatre history books.

My good fortune was with me again. Being at the Old Vic at the right moment in time, and the good fortune of having two friends to advise me like Ralph Richardson and Tony Guthrie. What's wrong with scoutmasters? Nothing. Especially when the scoutmaster is almost omniscient.

Imagination. Prey on the audience's imagination. Play with it like plasticine. Mould it, break it, remould it. Fashion it, shape it, let it free. Take them away with you. Weave tales and weave magic:

> *Think when we talk of horses that you see them*
> *Printing their proud hoofs i' the receiving earth;*
> *For 'tis your thoughts that now must deck our kings,*
> *Carry them here and there, jumping o'er times,*
> *Turning the accomplishment of many years*
> *Into an hour-glass . . .*

FIVE

MACBETH

We have each our private idea of Macbeth, Hamlet, Othello, Lear; we have all of us read of, if we have not seen great performances of these parts; so that every actor who undertakes them has to pass through a triple ordeal, encountering, first, our imagination, kindled by Shakespeare; second, our idealized memory of performances which used to please our, perhaps unripe, judgement; third, our conceptions of the great actors of the past, gathered from the often extravagant panegyrics of contemporaries. (William Archer, in *Brief Chronicles* by James Agate)

As an actor my initial view of *Macbeth* had been formed by the first part I'd played in it, that of Lennox. Later I was to see it through the eyes of Malcolm.

The first time I played the man himself was at the Old Vic in the 1937–38 season. I was just thirty, very fit, mentally very much in control and still bursting with ambition. I was full of confidence; I had played Hamlet at Elsinore and at the Old Vic, and I'd played Henry V as though the part had been written for me.

I think *Macbeth* is one of Shakespeare's best plays, and it is certainly one of my favourites. Shakespeare is always superb on the subject of death and on reactions to horrifying or terrifying news. To my mind 'Tomorrow and tomorrow' is as great a speech as 'To be or not to be'. *Macbeth* is compact, a perfectly

rounded piece. It tells a strong story at great speed and takes
the audience on a roller-coaster of excitement. You can see it a
hundred times and it will still appear fresh. It is visually superb,
which made me wonder what Shakespeare would have given us
had Hollywood existed in his time.

The play is beautifully paced for the leading actor, as witness
the England scene, which gives him time to relace his boots and
take some deep breaths, preparing himself for a thundering
finale, which I gave it, and which did not entirely meet with
James Agate's approval:

> Perhaps this is the place to say . . . and if it isn't I shall say
> it . . . that I have been more 'got at' over Mr Olivier's
> performance than by any other in my recollection. Chelsea
> semaphored, 'Unable conceive Macbeth as a gigolo.' Blooms-
> bury signalled, 'No use for Macbeth as a mountebank.' A
> young gentleman in corduroy trousers and velvet smoking
> jacket opined to my face that Macbeth should not be like
> a military colonel, retired. Reflecting that what the young
> gentleman needed was an active drill-sergeant, I proceeded
> to turn a deaf, but not altogether deaf, ear to another of
> the mincing brigade, who suggested that the new Macbeth
> shouted too loudly. I say not altogether deaf, because even
> the austerest critic is none the worse for knowing what is
> being said by the mob . . .

It had been a deliberate decision of mine to join the Old Vic
Company. I had approached them, and I knew that as far as they
were concerned I was quite a catch, for I had a movie star image
that was capable of filling a theatre. I also felt, and still do, that
you are judged entirely by your work in the classics. I wanted
to be taken seriously. I wanted to stand up and be counted. I
wanted to be conspicuous in the high court of the theatre. To
me, the Old Vic was the equivalent of the Old Bailey. Here I
would be judged for my classical work. Here I would pitch my
stand and stake my claim. Here I could ease my way into the
skin of the theatrical serpent, the skin that had been worn by
Burbage down to Irving and Barrymore. There it was, pressed

between the leather binding with the name William Shakespeare written on the spine. There it lay, waiting to be moulded, shaped, hurled in the air and back again.

The director of my 1937 *Macbeth* was Michel St Denis, a star director full of wit and imagination, though on this particular production neither seemed to be on our side. It was what you might call a stylized production. Everything in god-like proportions. The make-ups were mask-like. I had a huge false face on: a nose that went down straight from the forehead, a false chin and a putty forehead with vast eyebrows. The idea was to make something real through a highly poetic and unreal approach. I put myself entirely in St Denis's hands, but felt I was not good in such a theatrical production. I 'made up' to play Macbeth, instead of letting Macbeth play through me. I had everything outwardly and not enough inwardly. I think, in that production, Macbeth was nearer my sleeve than my heart.

Though I have relied a great deal on make-up and appearances over the years, I still maintain that the real look should come from inside. You cannot make up the lines by making up the face. It must come from the head and the heart first. What is added to it comes later. Remember the naked Greeks.

Everything seemed to be against us. At the dress rehearsal we reached cue three of the lighting plot at three o'clock in the morning. There was no way we were going to finish in time for the opening night. At this speed we'd still have been rehearsing at Christmas. They say there is a jinx on the play. I personally do not believe it, but at three o'clock that morning I think I might have been swayed. I remember Tony Guthrie coming down the aisle during one of the waits. There was a certain amount of glee showing in his walk. Perhaps 'glee' is too strong a word – more a feeling of 'told you so'. He spoke to St Denis and, as we all learned afterwards, the first night, which was to have been the next night, was cancelled.

It would be disastrous, Guthrie said, to keep the actors up all night and through the next morning, and expect them to appear before row after row of vultures dressed as penguins. So the first night did not happen.

Two nights later dear Lilian Baylis, founder of the Old Vic, died. Some say, and I do not disagree, that her death was brought on by the postponement of that first night. To my knowledge it was the first time it had ever happened at the Old Vic. Of course, for the superstitious, it was the play – what else could it be? But as far as I am concerned, it might just as well have been *Antony and Cleopatra*. It wasn't the play that killed her, it was the footlights that disturbed the might of that great lady. She towered above us all and departed quietly when her theatre was silenced.

We did open eventually, and not to a great deal of success – critically, that is – yet the box office did the best business the Vic had ever done up until that moment. In the end James Agate was not too unkind:

Since it would seem that, with the exception of Garrick, a great Macbeth has never been in the calendar, it is reasonable to expect that the new one should be lacking in perfect adequacy. It is a part demanding great natural and physical gifts, to which Mr Olivier at present can only oppose natural and physical shortcomings. He does not look like coping with Russian bears, Hyrcan tigers and rhinoceroses, whether armed or unarmed. His voice, which in the 'Tomorrow and tomorrow' and 'Sere and yellow leaf' speeches should vibrate like a cello, is of a pitch rather higher than the average. In other words, he is not a natural bass and has some difficulty getting down to baritone. All the same, he brings off some magnificent vocal effects, and his verse speaking has improved. Ideally, Macbeth might be likened to some oak, magnificent in outer shell but lacking in roots, and presently to be riven by the lightning of conscience. But nature has not so endowed Mr Olivier, who is forced to play the whole part nervously among the high tossed branches . . .

Mr Olivier will probably play this part twice as well when he has twice his present years. Meanwhile he registers another step in a career of considerable achievement and increasing promise.

Of course I was to play it again some years later, at Stratford in 1955, directed by Glen Byam Shaw, with a considerable amount of success. My voice was infinitely stronger and more powerful, and the greater experience of life which I had had since I first played the part really made a difference. The first time I had aged through pure imagination; now I could bring knowledge to bear. I was also happy with the make-up and the costumes. I found it was genuinely possible to make every second of Macbeth human, despite all that murdering of children. By luck, that second time I found a complete experience which belonged to the part, and I was able to get the right mixture of style and down-to-earth reality. I found the right ingredients in the right proportion.

I remember once discussing the part with Anthony Quayle, when we were both in *Titus Andronicus* behind the Iron Curtain. He had asked me if I was finding Titus tough going. 'It has', he said, 'all the hallmarks of a tough part.' 'Oh, God, yes,' I replied, 'but I suppose Macbeth is the worst, isn't it?' To which Quayle replied: 'No. Macbeth is positive, he knows what he is doing and he does it. He is a much jollier part altogether for the actor. Everybody flogs you every time they look at you as Titus. You are bemoaning your fate throughout and whatever happens to you is just another ghastly stroke of the knout, making you wail, "Oh, oh, oh, that this should happen to me." Othello's another part that's entirely composed of moaning, bellowing and scream-ing against fate. Macbeth is much more fun!' A sentiment I would agree with.

I don't know why my second Macbeth came together then, but like everything in this extraordinary work of theatre, it happened and it did. It was my moment. This has happened to me throughout my life. I have often been fortunate to have been in the right place at the right time. Blessed in that way. A sense of timing, almost an instinct. But then timing is made by the man, I think, and therefore man creates his own destiny. Take it or leave it, my timing was right, and I accept that with gratitude, whether it was man-made or God-made.

I was the right age for the production at Stratford, and at my peak: no mask-like make-up was required. I suppose it is an advantage when tackling all great roles if the age is right. Of course, this doesn't seem to happen with Romeo or with Lear. With Romeo you need the understanding of an adult and with Lear the physique of a younger man, though I did play Lear recently and didn't seem to do too badly.

Being the right age at Stratford was an enormous advantage. I had the bellows and I understood the play. Not that I didn't understand it before, but somehow I had grown into it.

SIX

RICHARD III

I think there is much that the public doesn't understand about acting. I think they understand baseball, cricket or football a great deal better. Let me try to explain. Naturally, if an actor is playing a baddie, no audience in the world likes him as much as they like the hero in the white hat, the man who makes them laugh or, best of all, the baddie who has them laughing with him. My ambition has been to lead the public away from the common trend of typecasting towards an appreciation of acting, so that they will come not only to see the play but also to watch acting for acting's sake.

Of the qualities I've just mentioned – the baddie, the hero, the comic – Richard of Gloucester has them all, which is what makes him, as it always has, such an attractive part to play. I mean, to be able to woo Lady Anne from hatred to acceptance in a five-minute scene is pure magic. There she is, on her way to bury her husband, whom Richard has killed, and he steps coolly in with, of all things, a proposal. The audacity is wonderful. To go from

LADY ANNE. *What black magician conjures up this fiend,*
To stop devoted charitable deeds?

to

    . . . 'Tis more than you deserve,
But since you teach me how to flatter you,
Imagine I have said farewell already.

Incredible to give an actor such a scene to play. And then to round it off by giving Richard:

> *Was ever woman in this humour woo'd*
> *Was ever woman in this humour won?*
> *I'll have her, but I will not keep her long.*

You can't wait to get on the stage to play it.

Contrary to what I've just said, I didn't want to do the play when it was first suggested. I didn't know the play all that well; all I knew was that Donald Wolfit had just made a critical success of the part (a performance, incidentally, which I did not see until some time later and then found disappointing). Whatever I did, I thought, would result in me being the loser. *Peer Gynt* and *Arms and the Man* were in the Old Vic repertoire at that time, 1944, and both were very successful – *Peer Gynt* sensationally so. Ralph Richardson knew what he was about. I got the feeling that I was being asked to do Richard III just to put me in my place. Looking back, I'm sure this wasn't so, but, like any other actor, I must be allowed my paranoia. Anyway, John Burrell and Ralph, my co-directors at the Old Vic, insisted that Richard was the ideal choice and there was nothing I could do about it except get on with it – so I did.

I began to study the piece and became more and more aware of what a part it was. It began to grow inside me. I had to find the character, and slowly he began to come to me. I had a picture of him in my head, a painting, an oil painting of what he ought to be like. I went around for some time with this visual image of him. I never believed that the real paintings of him were anything like him; or, if I did, I wasn't going to admit it. Nothing was going to stop me putting that make-up on. I wanted to look the most evil thing there was. But I also had to exercise some other fluid that would win Lady Anne. I decided to liberate in every pore of my skin the utmost libertinism I could imagine. When I looked at her, she couldn't look at me, she had to look away. And when she looked away, I would spend time devouring the region between her waist and upper thigh. Shocking maybe,

but right, I felt. It was right for my Richard, and he was becoming my Richard by the minute.

Problems have always spurred me to find a solution, I welcome them. As Richard III I had to make the audience like me. They must be won over by his wit, his brilliantly wry sense of humour.

The excitement was beginning; the adrenalin. An actor, when he begins to sense that he is on to something, is a bit like a stoat coming out of its hole and smelling the morning air: the nose twitches and the body starts to tingle. The flash of lightning away in the distance, the thunder still muted, but coming, slowly coming! Everything begins to change: the taste buds improve, the sense of smell is more acute, the mind is constantly wrapping itself round the image which is to be created, then presented to an unsuspecting public.

I didn't read any of the books that were around, protecting Richard from the false rumour written by this tinkerer with melodrama, whose name is William Shakespeare, who got it from someone else, who got it from someone else, who got it from someone else. I just stayed with the man himself:

> *Shine out, fair sun, till I have bought a glass,*
> *That I may see my shadow as I pass.*

Then there was the voice. It came to me: the thin reed of a sanctimonious scholar. I started putting it on at once. It arrived and set the vision going: thin and rapier-like, but all-powerful. Somewhere between the bridge of the nose and the sinuses at first. It was easy to pitch, and it was perfect for the three sides I have mentioned: the hero, the villain and the ironic comedian. It was a sound that helped me formulate the character. I think I tried it at the first reading – yes, I did. It was a bell ringing inside me: 'Now is the winter . . .' – scholarly, yet deadly. The perfect hypocrite. From the first few words you knew that this fellow was doubling up on himself. It had an edge that I had never used before, a mixture of honey and razor blades. I'm sure that if a serpent could converse with us rather than hiss, we would recognize a certain similarity. It seems to me that

even in a serpent's hiss there is a touch of a sexual smile. To
my mind that is what Shakespeare's Richard had: venom coated
with sugar. A veneer of smiling sophistication and wit, beneath
which lay the barb to hook the fish.

I suppose I must have heard the voice somewhere before,
maybe on a bus or a train, in a church or from a politician's
mouth – who knows? But there it is, and has remained to haunt
me ever since. It's amazing how many people have copied it. I
suppose I ought to be flattered . . . I think I am. A lot of young
actors, comedians, mimics – all over the top, in my opinion. If
I had used the voice that my impersonators credit me with, I
don't think the audience would have taken me too seriously.

Something significant happened to me a short time before I
played Richard. I was in Manchester playing Sergius in *Arms
and the Man*. One night, Tyrone Guthrie came to see it, and
after the show he and I began to walk back to the hotel together.
I remember the spot vividly: we were under the canopy at the
front of the opera house. I still think of it whenever I'm in
Manchester, walking to the studio from the Midland Hotel. He
stopped and said, 'Liked you very much.'

And I said, 'Thank you. Thanks very much.'

Hearing my tone, he asked, 'What's the matter? Don't you
like the part?'

To which I replied, 'Really, Tony, if you weren't so tall I'd hit
you.'

He then asked me, 'Don't you love Sergius?'

I replied, 'Are you out of your mind? How can you love a
ridiculous fool of a man like that?'

At which he observed, 'Well, of course, if you can't love him,
you'll never be any good as him, will you?' Words of wisdom. I
hadn't looked at it in that way before. It taught me a great
lesson. It kept echoing in my head: '. . . if you can't love him,
you'll never be any good as him.' Until then I'd never thought
of Guthrie in terms of teaching one how to act: I'd only thought
of him in terms of shoving people round you, or shoving you.
You know, placing people here or there, making a lot of movement. He directed purely by movement, it seemed to me. His
eye wasn't satisfied if something wasn't happening all the time,

whereas I believe there are times when there should be complete stillness.

Guthrie didn't direct *Richard*, John Burrell did; but Guthrie's remark had inched its way under my skin. I will always be grateful. In Manchester for the rest of the run I began to love Sergius, and my whole performance seemed to get better and better. For the rest of my life, I would apply this. When I came to it, I loved Richard and he loved me, until we became one.

As we moved nearer the first night, 26 September, the voice and the character fused. Richard went with me everywhere. There he was, sitting on my shoulder – or I on his. The portrait, my personal portrait, clear as a full moon in my head.

Actors (David Garrick) and playwrights (Colley Cibber) have tried to enhance the part over the years; Cibber's adaptation was the standard acting text for a century. 'Off with his head! so much for Buckingham!' is not Shakespeare. And when Hastings is arrested by *Cat*esby, *Rat*cliffe, and Lovel and says, 'The cat, the rat and Lovel our dog/rule all England under the hog', that's not Shakespeare but a contemporary doggerel which adds to the play's image of Richard. A rare Shakespearean event, when the part's the thing and not the play.

As an actor approaches a first night the sense of excitement is extraordinary. Like a bullfighter, everything is geared towards that moment, the moment of truth with his audience. One second of mistiming and it's over. One slip and they'll have you. Every waking minute the seconds are ticking away on your automatic time clock. You have gone into the countdown. As the last week approaches, anything that gets in the way of your train of thought is an irritation. An outside conversation (outside of the production, that is) is not welcome. Everything is homing in toward the raising of the curtain and, if you've got it right – or think you've got it right – you are not overconfident, but looking forward to the challenge. I could smell the play and couldn't wait to have it wrapped round me like a cloak. Waking in the morning, showering, shaving, bathing, it was there; the twinge in the gut, the knowledge that something was about to happen. I had no way of knowing it would be a success – there is no way of judging that – but I knew in my head that I had almost completed the jigsaw.

They say we are mere shadows. I like to think of the true actor as a skeleton. Bone, just bone, on to which he places and moulds the flesh, rather like a sculptor; but he has an advantage over the sculptor because his creation is animated. He, the actor, can play the author's tune. The image has been created, the vision has become reality and words will flow.

My optimism was not shared by the rest of the company. Looking back, I can still feel their sense of despair. The looks which said, '*Peer Gynt* is a sensational success . . . so is *Arms and the Man*, but *Richard* – ah, well – two out of three is not bad.' So I just carried on, head down, planning, plotting Richard himself. I think he might have been amused.

I wrote to Emlyn Williams and asked him if I could borrow his beautiful gag which gained him a marvellous laugh: when Buckingham goes too far, Richard III suddenly turns over the pages of his Bible very, very quickly. Emlyn wrote back, 'Delighted that you think it's worth copying.' There's quite a bit of legitimate borrowing in the theatre.

I thought, too, about stagecraft, about placing, about angles and lines. It was in this play that I used my back to telling effect. I've always worked with my back. If you have a scene with three people, place one and two just beyond midway up stage, then the third below them both, with his back to them; it's most effective, brings reality to what would otherwise be a rather unreal grouping, and makes a conversation piece. Of course you can't hold it for very long; eventually you have to move them around and change the pattern into some other agreeable shape. But it is an excellent method of bringing reality to a scene of three people who might otherwise be strung out across the stage in an unnatural straight line. Two can get down and the big shot stay up, but I think it works best if two can be up and the third stands below, with his back to them.

Suddenly we were there. A first night has its own evil presence. It is curious the things that will annoy and the things that don't. A professional is not annoyed by stage hands being noisy; they cannot help this if there have been many cuts and changes at the last moment, it's inescapable. Knowing the problems those boys are facing behind that backcloth or front-cloth, I just keep going straight on. Not being confident that you are word perfect is much more worrying.

Sometimes the audience gives such a feeling of friendly expectancy that they lift you to give a performance of tremendous verve: it's as if they are daring you not to fail; loving you to succeed. At others, they are leaden and seem to feel too much is being asked of their attentive powers. In a very big theatre it can be almost impossible to exert hypnotic influence: it is not possible to mesmerize more than a thousand people at a time. In February, you can face an absolute barrage of coughs as if the whole audience were a huge hospital for croup.

But this was the New Theatre, 26 September 1944. We were there and I was ready. Inside the dressing room I began to prepare. Over the tannoy I could hear the first trickle of the audience coming into the house. Nose on, wig on, make-up complete. There, staring back at me from the mirror, was my Richard, exactly as I wanted him. I'd based the make-up on an American theatre director called Jed Harris, the most loathsome man I'd ever met. My revenge on Jed Harris was complete. He was apparently equally loathed by the man who created the Big Bad Wolf for Walt Disney.

Make-up is a strange thing. I know that now it is not the fashion to wear it, but for me that's where a lot of the magic still lies. The smell of a stick of greasepaint – No. 5, No. 9, lake, 7½ – still makes my scalp tingle.

I stood up and again looked in the mirror. The monster stared back at me and smiled.

By now the house was filling up, chattering and laughing getting ready to gorge itself and spit out the bones of any actor not coming up to their measure of the role. Me . . . Richard smiled back at me again.

There was a spider somewhere inside my stomach, not a butterfly.

They say that an actor on a first night pumps enough adrenalin to kill an average person.

'Beginners, please.' One last look and then away.

It is a strange feeling standing behind the tabs waiting for that first moment of contact with the audience. Personally, I have never wanted to run away, but I understand people who have. There are some parts, few, but some, when you can't wait to unleash yourself on the audience, and this was one of them. I knew . . . and if they didn't agree with me, to hell with them.

I was in the slips and ready. The noise of the audience was still removed, but audible, which meant that the house lights were still up. I glanced around the stage. This was to be my world for the next three hours. Here I would plot, scheme, seduce and rise to the giddy heights of a crown. Here I would destroy Clarence, the Princes, Lady Anne, and cry for a horse in vain. I looked into the prompt corner and saw Diana Boddington, my stage manager, press the final bell for the bars. Far off I could hear it ringing.

Last questions: was I prepared? Of course I was. The spider in the stomach again. God, I should have gone to the lavatory. Deep breath . . . perfect. Control . . . control . . . everything geared to a fine edge, sharp as a razor . . . come on, get those tabs up, I've been here an hour.

I looked in the corner again. Diana pressed another button and the chatter in the front of house slowly ceased. The lights had dimmed and the warmers were on the curtains. Yet another switch and a green light winked. 'Now,' I thought. 'Now.' Up went the curtains and there we were: the audience and Richard, face to face for the first time.

The warmth from a full house is amazing. As the curtain rises, it rushes across the footlights like a great giant's breath. It fills your nostrils. Immediately you are bathed in the heat of the lights, alone and vulnerable.

'Now is the winter . . .' I was inside the skull, looking out through Shakespeare's eyes.

I had married parts of the end of *Henry VI Part III* with the opening soliloquy of Richard and so, instead of it lasting for a minute or thereabouts, it read for fully six.

Halfway through I knew. I knew that I was holding the reins. When I said, 'Can I do this and cannot get the crown?' the audience made a sort of 'hhhaaaa' sound. I knew it had worked

– whatever *it* was. They were mine for another hour before I need start worrying.

I remember being in the wings at one moment and saying to Beau (Nicholas) Hannen, 'Smell it, Beau? A funny smell – like oysters. Success.' I think he said, 'Yes.' At another moment I passed Diana in the corner: 'Do you smell it?'

'Yes, I do,' she replied. She knew these things instinctively. It was there, everywhere. The atmosphere was tingling. I had seduced Lady Anne and the audience as well.

It is on the second night that the reality of the first night is stamped indelibly on the brain. The second night audience comes, having been told by the newspapers and by their friends that they are going to see something special, so they are excited but relaxed . . . and rather smug that they have got a ticket.

The repertoire had three successes, and I had my Richard.

SEVEN

KING LEAR

When you've the strength for it, you're too young; when you've the age, you're too old. It's a bugger, isn't it? The Romeo syndrome in reverse. At least I had a crack at it at both ends of the scale. Pity I didn't play it at sixty as well. That would have been a great age, perhaps the perfect one.

I came to play Lear for the first time against my will. Ralph Richardson had an uncanny knack of claiming parts – he was a cunning old sod. What he'd do would be to play the part on the radio first, which was very popular in those days, television still being an infant at the party, and in this way establish a right to do it. He did this with *Cyrano de Bergerac*, which I very much wanted to play. He had been an enormous success on the radio with it and, therefore, it seemed only right that he should play it in the next season at the Old Vic.

I had to come up with a plan of campaign and, while rooting around in the more dastardly areas of my memory, something came to me. Ralph had once said to me that, although he felt he didn't really aspire to Shakespeare, there was one part he thought he could do and do well, and that was Lear.

I arranged to meet my co-directors, John Burrell and Ralph at the Old Vic to decide what we were going to do in the next season. We sat down and began to plan out the repertoire.

'I would like to play Cyrano,' said Ralph, knowing full well that I saw myself in the part.

'All right,' said Burrell, 'excellent.'

There was a pause and they looked at me. I waited for a moment and then, as though I'd had a sudden inspiration, I threw it in.

'Lear,' I said. 'I'd like to play Lear.'

Ralph blanched. He knew I'd done it out of pure villainy. 'Absolutely,' said Burrell. 'I certainly can't see anything against that, can you, Ralph?'

Poor old Ralph had to reply, 'No . . . no . . . no.' I'd got him.

The next day we went to the pub as usual for lunch, the Salisbury in St Martin's Lane. We sipped away for a bit and then, when I thought it the appropriate moment, I moved in.

'Good meeting yesterday, wasn't it?'

'Yes,' said Ralph.

'Pleased?'

'Very,' said Ralph.

'Think I'll make a good job of Lear?' I smiled at him. He didn't reply, he knew exactly what I was at. 'Why don't we swop?'

'What's that?' he asked.

'I'll give you Lear, if you give me Cyrano. Much better way round, don't you think?'

Those eyes searched into mine for a time, and then, very quietly, he said, 'No!'

I never thought for a moment he wouldn't swop; I thought it was just a formality. I didn't want to play Lear – well, not yet, anyway – but there it was, signed, sealed and delivered. He would play Cyrano, and his Lear would be taken care of on another occasion. Alas, it never was.

There was no turning back. Not only did I play Lear for the Old Vic, I directed it as well. No half measures for Olivier. If I was going to jump in, I might as well go the whole way. I was thirty-nine. We were still at the New Theatre in those days and, when we announced the production, the advance booking was phenomenal, and several hundred playgoers failed to get tickets for the first night. Perhaps they all wanted to come and see me fall on my bottom. Well, I didn't. Naturally there were comparisons: Donald Wolfit had recently played it, but then he never stopped playing it, and so had John Gielgud.

My production, when compared with Komisarjevsky's, did not come out favourably, but then it's a hell of a play to direct and play the leading part as well. Looking back, perhaps I should have left the directorial side to someone else, but I was flying high in those days.

I always start studying a part at once. First I exercise my chords and my chord muscles by shouting full out in the open air, probably to an audience of cows. I try to extend my vocal range and make sure I can manage eight or more lines without pausing for breath. Then I practise the role in detail to myself. It is a great mistake to take up rehearsal time with technical matters. By the first rehearsal of *Lear* I knew exactly where to take a breath, how to light and shade my voice, and how to tonalize it at certain moments in order to get the utmost variety. The actor must keep an audience engaged by constant changes of inflections; he must keep them forward in their seats; he must have an acute sense of when he is boring them, when they are about to yawn or look at their watches, wondering when the interval is coming; he must know the instant he has lost their interest.

When I get to the actual rehearsal I like to work full out, to try my complete range, so that I can eventually produce my final performance by a process of selection.

In my production I made the court appear one that was well used to the sudden whims of Lear and his passion for authority. I made him finicky, almost childlike, and the court was prepared to humour him. I set this up before my first entrance, so when I made my appearance I was able to cast a critical and fussy eye over the dress and position of my guards. I think by doing this I gave the part more plausibility.

I suppose my performance might have leant a little more towards Gielgud's than Wolfit's. Wolfit stressed the senility of the character, whereas in mine the octogenarian's body still pulsed with life and passion. I was able to get tremendous power vocally, so in the storm scene the thunder and lightning were in the King himself as well as in the elements. I felt that one of the greatest moments in my performance was my distraction before the storm: 'A tremendous tantrum of impotence,' Ken

Tynan called it, 'full of crazed emphases and teasing fullness of tone.'

> *I will have such revenges on you both*
> *That all the world shall – I will do such things, –*
> *What they are yet I know not, – but they shall be*
> *The terrors of the earth . . .*

Audrey Williamson said,

> . . . the sheer torrential sound of it swept across the senses like Niagara, but in all this raving music one could still hear the tortured cry of a drowning man. The sudden drop of the voice at 'O Fool, I shall go mad', clutching at the jester for support and wild, broken flight from the scene wrung the heart as no other Lear at this moment has succeeded in doing. (*Old Vic Drama*, 1946–7)

Most kind of the critics. It's always heartwarming when someone else says it. It was actually an extremely successful production and I came out of it with a great deal of credit, which I think surprised several people and was an added bonus to me since I hadn't wanted to do it in the first place.

Frankly Lear is an easy part, one of the easiest parts in Shakespeare apart from Coriolanus. We can all play it. It is simply bang straightforward. Not like Romeo for instance, where you spend the whole evening searching for sympathy. But then anyone who lets an erection rule his life doesn't deserve much sympathy, does he?

No, Lear is easy. He's like all of us really, he's just a stupid old fart. He's got this frightful temper. He's completely selfish and utterly inconsiderate. He does not for a moment think of the consequences of what he has said. He is simply bad-tempered arrogance with a crown perched on top. He obviously wasn't spanked by his mother often enough. It is crass stupidity that governs him. I mean, to turn away from his favourite daughter like that, what kind of an idiot is he? Mind you, I suppose Shakespeare knew what he was about; by getting Cordelia off the stage he was able to save the management money. In his day the boy actor who played Cordelia would double as the fool. That makes rather interesting ripples through the piece, does it not?

That first production at the New Theatre I enjoyed enormously. It didn't tire me, although the pundits always say it's the most exhausting role in Shakespeare. Nonsense: I disagree. Of course I had youth and vigour on my side, but not for a moment did I find it tiring. I enjoyed every performance thoroughly. Of course I had to wear the age on my sleeve and, looking now at some of the photographs in close-up, I suppose I did look a little like Clapham Junction, but I'm certain the overall appearance and interpretation were well worth a ticket.

Naturally with energy on my side I was able to give 'Blow, winds, and crack your cheeks!' everything that my bellows allowed. I was determined to be heard in Trafalgar Square and I'm sure the effect was electric, for I stood in jet blackness shot through with lightning. It was only later, when I came to play the part again, that I realized such excess wasn't necessary. Age teaches you that. Age gives you the authority anyway. Something well worth remembering when tackling the part: you do not quake and quaver and nod like a toy dog in the back of a car with age. Age is something else. Age has a dignity, almost a serenity, and when anger comes from age it does not have to be shouted. It explodes with authority. A look, a smile can be just as chilling. Of course Lear has to rage, I'm not denying that, but it's well worth looking at how much vocal anger is necessary. The austere command of years can be conveyed just as powerfully, perhaps even more so, if played with steely calm.

I suppose one of the reasons why people say it is an exhausting role is that it is usually played by an elderly actor. The audience spend most of the evening on the edge of their seats fearing that the performer will have a seizure at any moment. They are breathless with anticipation. Was that stumble part of the action or was it real? When he put his hand to his heart, was it to feel if it was still in motion? Was that a crack of the voice or was it the beginnings of the death rattle? This is cruelty, the poor old man shouldn't be forced to do it. The management should be reported to the Royal Society for Prevention of Cruelty to Aged Actors.

At the end of the evening, when the ancient star inches his way down to the centre of the stage and nods his tired head towards his exhausted public, he does not realize that the appreciation, the tumultuous applause, the accolades that are hurled towards his deaf ears are not for his rendering of the Bard's great lines, but come out of relief that he is still standing and has not left for the great Green Room in the sky.

Of course he is shattered, and of course it is the most exhausting part in Shakespeare. The poor old darling nearly dies every night, but he loves it. Try and stop him doing it, just try.

There is nothing more tempting than to hang on to the curtain at the end of a long evening and let the audience know that you have given your all for them, just for them. This was the night and the only night when you sweated blood to give them the definitive performance. Tonight you and they shared something special. This performance was for their grandchildren. You know the bow, we've all done it. It goes something like this:

Eyes take in the gallery, hold for a moment.

Eyes take in the upper circle, hold for another moment.

Eyes to the dress circle, longer hold, more money here.

Eyes to the stalls, even longer.

Then to the left and to the right, for the boxes. Treat the boxes as if there was Royalty seated in them.

Then slowly let the head come completely down, chin almost on chest. Play the modesty.

Then the questions.

Is this really for me? This applause that I hear, it can't be for me?

I can't believe it. What have I done to deserve this? I am only a mere player, your humble servant.

Wait for a moment, then play the modesty, again. Arms outstretched to the company on either side. Without them, dear audience, without my fellow players, I am nothing.

Wait for another beat and then move forward.

Hand on heart, then final bow.

I would stay with you longer my dear audience, but I am exhausted. I must leave you now.

By this time they should be on their feet. If not you've got something wrong.

My God, those old actors knew how to do it!

One of the first productions of *Lear* I saw was in Los Angeles, when I was living there before the war. It was given by an actor called Randle Ayrton, who was then a famous British star. He was with the Stratford-upon-Avon company, and they took this particular production of *Lear* out to the States. It was considered quite a good production. I went to see it with my mother-in-law, who knew him. I was still married to Jill Esmond at the time. We went backstage afterwards to bandy the compliments and exchange the usual pleasantries. My mother-in-law gushed all over him.

'You were just like the Old Man,' she said. 'Just like the Old Man.'

Irving even then, so long after his death, was still referred to as the Old Man. Of course he was; he'd based it on him, hadn't he?

Listening to the compliments flying, I came to a decision. I vowed to eradicate all knowledge of the Old Man from the public's memory forever. I was determined to become the Old Man myself. Let them impersonate me fifty years after my death. My will was granite. I was determined to be the greatest actor of all time.

My last performance of *Lear*, made for television in 1983, I must leave for you to judge. It was not geared for theatre, though of course its origins were there. Strangely enough I still didn't find it exhausting.

I was thinking the other day of Shakespeare's own basic description of all his tragedies. Surprisingly enough it is said by the one man who could not make up his mind, but who really knew how to say something. Such a brain.

HAMLET. *So, oft it chances in particular men,*
That for some vicious mole of nature in them,
As, in their birth — wherein they are not guilty,

Since nature cannot choose his origin, –
By the o'ergrowth of some complexion,
Oft breaking down the pales and forts of reason;
Or by some habit, that too much o'er-leavens
The form of plausive manners; that these men
Carrying, I say, the stamp of one defect,
Being nature's livery, or fortune's star,
Their virtues else, be they as pure as grace,
As infinite as man may undergo,
Shall in the general censure take corruption
From that particular fault: The dram of evil
Doth all the noble substance of a doubt,
To his own scandal.

Well, there's your Richard, there's your Hamlet, there's your Macbeth, there's your Othello . . . and your Lear.

Sometimes I wonder if I have not become a little like Lear myself. Is it now possible that I have placed a part of his clothing upon me? I wear an invisible theatrical crown, which I like, am very attached to and will not give up. Just as I was determined to eliminate Irving and let the Old Man's spotlight rest on me, the Young Man, now I have in turn become the Old Man and somebody somewhere must be thinking the same thoughts that I had in Hollywood all those years ago. Well, whoever you are and wherever you are, if you want it, you'll have to come and get it. But I warn you, it will take more than physical strength and cunning to get it. First you have to dust clean the blackboard of the chalk of memory. But begin, whoever you are, do begin. You must, if you believe, and you will not succeed if you do not believe. But just remember, as you come tiptoeing along the passageway to the chamber of gold, that you will find an old man standing at the entrance, legs apart, back straight and erect, eyes piercing, barring the way.

EIGHT

OTHELLO

When it was announced that I was going to run the National Theatre Company, a letter arrived on my desk one morning from Kenneth Tynan, then drama critic of *The Observer*. Tynan had not endeared himself to me over the years, because he had constantly attacked Vivien Leigh for her performances, which I found quite unjustified. Vivien was a very fine actress, as can be witnessed still in films like *Gone with the Wind* and *A Streetcar Named Desire*. But it seems to me that the critics have never been able to accept beauty and talent. You can have one or the other, not both. She had both.

As far as Tynan was concerned, she could do no right, and this I found offensive. It is so easy to attack, much easier than to praise, and Tynan's pen was brilliant and often dipped in acid. As it happened, he was always generous towards me, which didn't help when Vivien and I were performing together. There is little joy in getting a good review when your other half is getting a bad one. But apart from his blindness towards Vivien, it has to be said that he was one of the finest dramatic critics of the twentieth century: I put him up there alongside Shaw. His premature death was a great loss to the arts in general, for, whether criticizing or merely being involved, he was a major influence on what has now become our modern theatre.

His letter that morning simply said that he was prepared to give up his Fleet Street world if I would take him into the National as literary adviser; he wanted to join the other side of the footlights. As you can imagine, I was very surprised. I arranged a lunch and we talked. Ken became my dramaturge.

What has this got to do with Othello? One of the conditions that Ken gave me was his insistence that, within five years of his joining us, I would perform the role. It had never occurred to me. Iago was the big part, as far as I was concerned. I had already played Iago and really didn't fancy approaching the play from the other fellow's point of view. If I take on Othello, I told Ken, I don't want a witty Machiavellian Iago. I want an honest-to-God NCO.

I'd played Iago with Ralph Richardson the first time round. Poor Ralph, he was not born to play the Moor. His Othello was as boring an Othello as has ever been, and I was in like a jackdaw, stealing the goodies. I played Iago entirely for laughs. No menace, no danger at all. I thought, rather than play him like a sixteenth-century villainous character, it would be more interesting and acceptable to play him terribly sweet, and as charming as can be. I felt that he would seem more dangerous and plausible this way, and that everybody would believe him 'honest Iago'. And I played up to it. I believed that that's what people thought I was – honest. Then, when I got to the soliloquy, I'd have my syringe ready and let the audience have it straight up the arse.

It didn't work critically, but it did work for me. And, of course, it didn't work for poor old Ralph.

So, when it was suggested that I play the Moor, I naturally had reservations knowing, as I did, the play from Iago's point of view. I felt that Othello was a loser from the word go. I had this fantasy, and I like to think that it's probably very near the truth, that Shakespeare and Burbage went out on a binge one night, each trying to outdrink the other, the yards of ale slipping down their throats and thickening their tongues. Just before one or other slid under the alehouse table, Burbage looked at Shakespeare and said, 'I can play anything you write – anything at all.' And Shakespeare said, 'Right, I'll fix you, boy', and wrote Othello for him. I'm sure something like that must have occurred.

It's a very badly designed role; for instance, there are too many climaxes, far too many. Working on the assumption that

Othello's first reaction to Iago is, 'Come on, I know you're after Cassio's lieutenancy . . . I'll get the truth out of you – come on', this starts Othello on a higher step than Iago. But in getting the truth, Othello trips himself up, becomes jealous without being aware of how it began, and goes completely over the edge. He rants, he roars like a cornered bull, the barbs hanging from his neck, blood dripping, waiting for the *coup de grâce.*

In the middle act there are some very fine pieces: 'Like to the Pontic sea', and the 'Farewell plumed troops' speeches. But soon come the fits and the raging again, saying things like 'I'll tear her to pieces, chop her up into messes' – all demanding you to scream at your utmost.

It is very easy to show off and bellow away like a dying moose. 'Look at me, audience, I can bellow mightier than anyone has bellowed before.' How often, as a beginner, one has done it, bludgeoning an audience into defeat. Bursting eardrums with the throttle full out, big is beautiful. In the last scene you kill Desdemona – a huge peak – followed by two or three tremendous outbursts in a very short space of time. At your death, the quiet sigh of the audience, 'Thank God . . . thank God . . .' and they leave, scratching behind the ears.

No, I thought, this is one hell of a difficult part. It's Iago's piece. There he is, the beast, sitting on your shoulder and quietly winking at the audience. But all this said, the challenge was out. Tynan had insisted and, let's face it, there's nothing more flattering for an actor, no matter how much he has achieved.

One of the innermost, and at the same time overtly conscious, determinations of my life has always been to make the modern generation understand what I am doing. I knew I could not play Othello in any detached way: I would have to put every single throb of my tiniest vein right into it. I knew I would not be able to fulfil myself in the part, or the part in myself, unless I did this. It was not a role I would be able to rid myself of when I took off the make-up. I would have to start quietly, to come on to the stage first as the most real person the audience had ever seen, then, bit by bit, when I'd won their confidence, I would be able to start riding them. Only then would they accept my

roaring. Through careful timing and delicate use of rhythm I
would give the audience seconds, moments, tiny instances of
recognition of the absolute truth of the situation. By absolute
spontaneous reaction I would make the audience feel illuminated,
not by a *new* sensation but by a half-suspected sensation of truth
that they had only subconsciously been aware of before. When
that happened it would be like a flashing mirror for them. But I
would have to work hard to achieve such an effect.

I would not care if people tittered when I rolled around on the
floor in what critics would be bound to call the wrong place,
because I would know that the audiences were building up to a
much larger dose of catharsis later on. If I roared and screamed
and behaved grotesquely and the audience laughed, I would
know I'd relieved their tension. They'd come back better for
the end, more tragically receptive.

I began to think about the play again, and look at it from
Othello's point of view. I began to sniff around the man, like
an old dog viewing yesterday's bone. I began to read the play
and re-read it, worming my way into the text. Scratching
at the veneer I had left on it from my previous experience
of Iago's point of view, chipping away and getting back to the
bare fresh page, throwing off the harness of a previous production.

To create a character, I first visualize a painting; the manner,
movement, gestures, walk, all follow. It began to come. Pictures
and sounds began to form in my mind, subconsciously at first,
but slowly working their way to the surface. You keep the image
in your heart and then project it on to the oil painting. I say 'oil'
rather than 'watercolour' because, for me, acting will always be
in oils.

I was beginning to know how I should look: very strong. He
should stand like a strong man stands, with a sort of ease,
straight-backed, straight-necked, relaxed as a lion. I was certain
that he had to be very graceful. I was sure that, when he killed
in battle, he did it with absolute beauty.

Black . . . I had to *be* black. I had to feel black down to my
soul. I had to look out from a black man's world. Not one of
repression, for Othello would have felt superior to the white

man. If I peeled my skin, underneath would be another layer of black skin. I was to be beautiful. Quite beautiful.

Throwing away the white man was difficult, but fascinating. Of course, you can never truly do this, but there were times when I convinced myself that I had. The oil painting.

A walk . . . I needed a walk. I must relax my feet. Get the right balance, not too taut, not too loose. Walk with poise. It wasn't working. I couldn't make it work. The movement, the rhythm that I needed wasn't there. I watched, I studied – nothing. I should walk like a soft black leopard. Sensuous. He should grow from the earth, the rich brown earth, warmed by the sun. I took off my shoes and then my socks. Barefooted, the movement came. Slowly it came; lithe, dignified and sensual. Lilting yet positive.

I felt that Othello spoke quite differently from any other character in Shakespeare: he speaks like a foreigner who's learnt the language too carefully. His moral attitude is also that of somebody who has studied to impress. The Senate think he is clear, pure, full of cool courage. He's concocted this perfect cocoon exterior: he is the statue of a perfect man. But the statue is flawed: Shakespeare gives him one fissure. The fissure cracks and the statue breaks. He is too jealous: the fault is self-deception. He's the greatest exponent of self-deception there's ever been. Othello's self-conscious dramatization of himself as the noble warrior leads him to ignore reality.

The voice. I was sure he had a deeper voice than mine. Bass, a bass part, a sound that should be dark violet – velvet stuff. A careful way of speaking, a Moor who didn't speak Venetian naturally. A bell . . . sometimes your body can become a bell. A superbly shaped instrument for sounds to be echoed round, shaped, then sent soaring away toward the attentive ear.

The voice was of great importance. I began to work on it every day. I had to lower it, and slowly I surely did.

I was becoming the text. I was forgetting Iago, 'honest Iago'.

I gave a full-blooded, all-out rendering of the part at the very first rehearsal and from then on I tried out things extravagantly, way over the top. Hands, eyes, body, a kind of self-flagellation.

I have done this most of my acting life, grasping the nettle early on and making a fool of myself.

The company realize right away how embarrassing it's going to be and I save a hell of a lot of time. I am not doing it for the company. If you are frightened of making a fool of yourself, if you start too subtly, too cosily, just giving little glimpses of what the part might become, you create huge barriers for yourself later on. You must be open, naïve, prepared to charge down every alley that presents itself, until you lock into the ones that you and your character need.

Often, by mistake, you'll stumble on something, and it will be exactly what you want and you hold on to it, keep it and cherish it. Often an accident happens and there it is: the man, the man you want. That's him.

In the handkerchief scene, I intended angry insistence. It developed into imploring anger. It was right.

Then the rose: I did not whip Iago's face with it, but stroked him gently as much as to say, 'Come on, you're pulling my leg. I'm not for that.' Othello wasn't so simple that he couldn't tell when Iago was being a bit of a humbug. It was an absolutely realistic touch, which the audience appreciated.

On the other hand, you mustn't let this self-indulgence carry you away. As I said earlier, this is a pitfall that can become a bearpit. Once in, never to be seen again. You must always be like a jockey on a racehorse, knowing the slightest movement, change of balance, will disturb the machinery. On the other hand, you must let the horse know where he is going, where you want him to go, not where he wants to go. Bit between his teeth and he'll return to the stable, not the winning post. You hold on to the reins, guiding subtly, never letting the neck stretch out. Always keeping something back.

It doesn't matter how big the acting is, how loud you're roaring, but it must never be absolutely at the top of your range. If you hit the ceiling then you let the audience see the measure of you, and you're done for. You look weak, instead of strong, and they think, 'He's straining himself . . .', and you're finished. Always keep something in the reserve tank.

An audience will encourage you to show the extent of your

powers, willing you and wooing you to do so, but an audience is like Iago himself: once having got you to open your heart, it will eat your entrails. You, the actor, must always be on top. Show a glimpse, flirt, live dangerously, but never take your trousers off. Let them think that you are always just about to. Let them beg. Let them come back for more. Always the encore.

So the ranting and roaring did take place, but only in the confines of the rehearsal room. Those four walls splattered with the blood and tears of actors past and present, fingering their way skyward like striped trees on an autumn backcloth. I roared, I ranted, I embarrassed my fellow players. I honed and hewed, and fought with William Shakespeare. Round after round, some days losing bitterly, some days with a glimmer of what might be. Words coming, words going. Some days not a syllable could be remembered. Other days everything as clear as daylight.

Working on the voice, lowering it, lowering it.

Getting more used to the feel of the rehearsal room floor through bare feet. Knowing what it was like to be at one with the bare boards, the earth beneath, the sky above. Slowly moving towards the opening. The play becoming less of a play at times and more of a reality. Moments when I think I am Othello, when I am convinced I am black.

Beware . . . I tell myself to beware. Come back to the text, do not drift. You are only good if you are in control. Every moment you must be in complete control.

Sometimes I begin to think that Shakespeare is playing Iago and I am playing Burbage.

On the first night, I was in the theatre several hours before, creating the image which now looked back at me from the mirror. Black all over my body, Max Factor 2880, then a lighter brown, then Negro Number 2, a stronger brown. Brown on black to give a rich mahogany. Then the great trick: that glorious half yard of chiffon with which I polished myself all over until I shone. Pancake make-up looks powdery and, when you sweat, it is apt to break out in little rivulets if you aren't careful, but if you use this wonderful bit of chiffon, it gleams a smooth ebony. The lips blueberry, the tight curled wig, the white of the eyes, whiter than ever, and the black, black sheen that covered my flesh and bones, glistening in the dressing-room lights.

RODERIGO. . . . *Never tell me; I take it much unkindly*
That thou Iago, who hast had my purse
As if the strings were thine, shouldst know of this . . .

Roderigo's first lines came echoing over the tannoy. The curtain was up.

Deep breaths, stand like a strong man stands with a feline ease. Straight-backed, straight-necked, relaxed as a lion. Kill with beauty . . .

I am . . . I am, I . . . I am Othello . . . but Olivier is in charge. The actor is in control. The actor breathes into the nostrils of the character and the character comes to life. Othello is my character for this moment in my time – he is mine. He belongs to no one else, he belongs to me. When I sigh, he sighs. When I laugh, he laughs. When I cry, he cries.

Remember, do not show them the complete iceberg. Do not let them scratch behind the ears. Keep them there, riveted, until you decide to let them go. Hold them in the palm of your hand. Your pink palm. How pink it seems when framed with black . . .

Black skin – white costume – red rose . . . the first line comes.

'Tis better as it is.

Dear Ken, your contract is fulfilled . . .

NINE

ANTONY AND CLEOPATRA

In 1951 I had the St James's Theatre and was talking to Roger Furse one day about what we should do next. Roger was a brilliant designer, and he and I had worked together for years and indeed continued to do so until I formed the National Theatre in 1963.

'I really can't imagine,' he said, 'why you and Vivien don't do *Antony and Cleopatra* and *Caesar and Cleopatra* in repertoire.'

It hadn't occurred to me before, but the more I thought about it the better the idea seemed. I knew Vivien would be wonderful in the Shaw, but I wasn't so certain about the Shakespeare. As it turned out I needn't have had any worries at all. She was brilliant, and in my opinion the best Cleopatra ever. She was radiant and beautiful and shone through the lines as if they had been specially written with her in mind. My Antony was not bad either, though some critics didn't seem to agree with me. But at this period in my career it didn't matter, Vivien and I were sailing, we were set in the galaxy, and fortunately everyone wanted to see us. There was a tremendous feeling of optimism in the air. The war had been over for six years, we had grown used to peace, there was a Festival of Britain on the South Bank, the population seemed to be on an upward surge, and Vivien and I were twinkling above it. Within a week of announcing the forthcoming productions at the St James's we were sold out for the twenty-six-week run and were thinking about going to America.

I'd never really thought a lot about Antony, as a person that is. I mean really he's an absolute twerp, isn't he? A stupid man. But thank God Shakespeare didn't try to rectify that; if he had, there would have been no play. Not a lot between the ears has Antony. Now Cleopatra, she's the one. She has wit, style and sophistication, and if played well, no Antony, however brilliant, can touch her. There she stands, the golden Queen of the Nile, towering above the play and toying with her soldier lover. She has the good sense not to tell him of his shortcomings, but then why should she? It was a purely physical relationship. Two very attractive human beings determined to do wonderful things to each other. Result . . . suicide. There is nothing cerebral about their love: it is pure passion, lust and enjoyment. And why not? How would you feel alone in a chamber with that lady? I don't think you'd want to discuss *The Times* crossword. You'd keep inclemency to the bedroom and not use it as an adjective to describe the clouds outside.

So there he is, little Antony, Julius's friend of twenty years earlier, grubbing around the Nile and making a cock-up of everything. The young man who had orated so brilliantly over Caesar's body now a middle-aged lap-dog. I often wonder what the relationship was between Caesar and Antony. I think one of Antony's problems was that because he was a nobleman, he thought he would automatically have an honourable character, but he hadn't. The greatest and the noblest he wasn't. But what a fantastic final speech, wonderful last lines. Strangely enough they make me weep to say them now.

> . . . *the greatest prince of the World,*
> *The noblest; and do now not basely die,*
> *Not cowardly put off my helmet to*
> *My countryman; a Roman by a Roman*
> *Valiantly vanquished. Now my spirit is going;*
> *I can no more.*

Haunting, quite haunting. As I say, they make me weep now, but I never wept on stage.

Though I call him a twerp, it's still a great part. You've got to see that it is and follow it through. The one thing you mustn't do is play it for sympathy; this you must beware of, and it's a very easy trap to fall into. Once you try to wheedle your way into the audience's pocket you've had it. You may as well pick up your toga and go home. The actor should remember to leave the heroics in the forum in the other play with Caesar's body. This Antony is very different.

I once had the chance to play the Antony in *Julius Caesar*, but only for a brief moment and not completely. It was many years ago, when I was with the Lena Ashwell players – the 'Lavatory Players' as I christened them, because we played town halls and swimming baths where the only changing rooms seemed to be the lavatories. *Julius Caesar* was to be my last play with them. During the run of it I was asked to take my talents elsewhere, having been dismissed for disorderly conduct on stage, as I explain in *Confessions of an Actor*.

I was playing the part of Flavius, not exactly the most taxing role in the world, and Crowds. You've got to have Crowds in *Julius Caesar* no matter how small. Somehow I don't think I was a very good Crowd, for I spent most of my time trying to make the other actors giggle, which of course eventually led to my downfall.

There we were, sitting in our cubicles, waiting to bring the Bard to whoever came to that particular swimming pool that night. Can you imagine going along with your bathers and towel tucked under your arm only to discover that the water had been boarded up for the evening and atop it were Lena Ashwell's bonny band of troupers? I think we'd have been better off performing an aqua show. The acoustics were wonderful if you didn't mind the echo, echo, echo. And the scenery, as you can imagine, was minimal. As I say, there we were sitting in our cubicles like seals in the slips waiting to give our all in front of a handful of deaf pensioners and exploding children who were only too well aware how their own little foghorns could echo back to them, when it was discovered that our leading man (Godfrey Kenton), who was playing Antony, hadn't turned up. All eyes to the understudy – me.

'Larry, Godfrey's not here.'

'Not here?'
'Not here.'
'Ah.'
'Do you know it?'
'Backwards . . . and Brutus and Cassius . . .'
'Well you're playing Antony until he gets here . . . forwards.'
'What about Flavius?' For whom I was already toga'd.
'Flavius too. Act one beginners, please.'
I went out in front of the swimming-pool patrons and began:

FLAVIUS. *Hence! home, you idle creatures, get you home . . .*

You can imagine the sort of reaction that had. I finished the
scene, somewhat hurriedly I imagine, then moments later re-
appeared as Antony. I had gone up in stature, stepped out of
the crowd and into the breach.

Not a bad part, Antony, but he doesn't really come into his
own until the forum scene. Until then the character is just
warming up, getting ready for the big oratory. Caesar was duly
killed and my big moment was almost upon me. I was really
looking forward to it. Let me get at it. I'll stir those nodding
zombies in the front row. They'll tell their grandchildren they
heard Olivier's 'Friends, Romans, countrymen . . .'

I was about to begin. What a speech, I was going to ring it out
round the pool from the top diving board to the back of the empty
balcony. I was going to play it so well that it would remain in
the heads of those who witnessed it forever. Stories would be told
years hence of this night when Antony came alive in a swimming pool. People who had not been there would pretend that
they had:

I was there that night when young Olivier stepped in and gave
us the definitive Antony. I knew then that a star was born. It
must have been the same feeling as witnessing the first
performance of Irving in *The Bells* or Kean as Shylock. I knew
a major actor had arrived. When he began his big speech, the
atmosphere was electric, the hairs stood up on the back of
my neck as I became aware that I was seeing something very

special. What a privilege to have been there at that moment. I will never forget it . . .

Suddenly I looked into the wings and there was this frantic tic-tac man. It was Godfrey. He'd arrived and was dressed and was wanting to come on. For a moment I thought of refusing to leave. I mean, what could he do, what could anybody do for that matter? I was there, I was in possession of the boards, I could squat and only a hook would get me off. It seemed such a shame to deny the audience the magic that I was prepared to give them. More frantic arm moving from the wing. Should I deny not only them but also their grandchildren who would sit on their laps in fifty years' time and hear the story? Surely my duty was to posterity.

'Get off, it's my turn.'

Another beat . . . a pause . . . very tempting . . .

'Get off..' The whisper was getting louder.

What the hell . . . I'll play it another time . . . I'll show them. But of course I never did. Slowly I made my exit. A new shape and voice took over the role and I went back into the Crowd, and I don't believe that any of those nodding geriatric gnomes or nose-picking adolescents noticed. They were dreaming of days gone by or days to come and the mighty Caesar was forgotten for ever.

So you see, I knew something of the early Antony when I came to play the later one.

I decided not to direct when we did *Antony and Cleopatra* at the St James's. I felt that acting in both plays would be enough without the hassle of the production as well, so Michael Benthall undertook the direction, and did a fine job.

I gave Vivien one note or tip on the first rehearsal. 'Darling, do me a favour,' I said, 'just try and lower your voice a whole octave.' And she did. Something I did myself as Othello. She lowered her voice and it captured the performance. Something she was to do again later when she played *Streetcar*.

After her success in the Shaw, the press were waiting. Her real tussle is to follow, they said, for Shaw makes the most brilliant comic role for Cleopatra in the first act, but after the middle of the play she doesn't get one laugh. He loses interest in Cleopatra and fastens his interest on Caesar; he just adores Caesar. Bad playwriting. But it happens occasionally to authors that they create a part, lose interest and throw the proportions of all the other aspects. But Vivien surmounted this problem and made it in the Shakespeare part too; she made it with top honours. They had underestimated the lady, she was brilliant. As I have said, it was as though the Bard had picked up his pen and for a moment looked down the centuries and seen her. The gods had given him a glimpse of four hundred years on; down at the end of the telescope he had seen Vivien dancing.

I think the vocal note was the only one I gave her. She knew how to play the part. She seized it, fashioned and formed it, then showed us the magic.

Looking back at this chapter, it must seem that I have brushed Antony aside by calling him a twerp. This does not mean that it is still not a great part. It is, it is a wonderful part and one which I look back upon with relish. I really wouldn't have missed him for the world. There are glorious passages of writing and poetry. It's a hell of a part to play. His final two scenes, the one with Eros and then the one with Cleopatra, wonderful moments of poetic tragedy.

ANTONY. *Since Cleopatra died,*
I have liv'd in such dishonour, that the gods
Detest my baseness. I, that with my sword
Quarter'd the world, and o'er green Neptune's back
With ships made cities, condemn myself to lack
The courage of a woman . . .

Not bad, eh? His use of language is staggering. His descriptions are deadly accurate and used with such economy. A great, great gift.

It's a wonderful part. But just remember, all you future Antonys, one little word of advice: Cleopatra's got you firmly by the balls.

TEN

THE MERCHANT OF VENICE

My Shylock owed more to Benjamin Disraeli than to Fagin, physically and mentally. There was to be no stropping of knives on the soles of shoes, no fingering the sharpness of the blade, no splitting hairs with the curved edge, no spitting oaths on to the courtroom floor, no rolling eyes to the deaf gods.

I was determined to maintain dignity and not stoop physically and mentally to Victorian villainy. Not for me the long, matted hair, invariably red, the hooked nose and the bent back. I had got all that out of my system playing A. B. Raham in Somerset Maugham's *Home and Beauty*. That image of Shylock I had always seen as a caricature and an easy way out, not only making mock of the Jewish race but also of Shakespeare himself. He is too good a writer to be dealt with in that way, though over the centuries it has been a popular way of performing the part: the red wig begging to be hissed from the gallery, the more boos the better; the audience backing Gratiano, that embryonic Fascist.

I wanted to find something else – again the old search for reality. In this I was greatly helped by Jonathan Miller, my director at the National Theatre in 1970. First of all I wanted to find a setting for *The Merchant of Venice* which would give it a feeling of dignity and austerity. I hit upon 1880–1885, that period when the Victorians had found their maturity. Tall hats and frock coats, a time of clean and polished fingernails. Fortunately Jonathan and my other associates agreed with my vision.

In the early days of rehearsal I remember Jonathan being

ruthless in his criticism of some of my line readings. It came as
quite a shock to begin with, until I slowly began to realize what
he was at.

'You're not going to say it like that, are you?' Echoes of
Guthrie.

'Why not?'

'Can't you think of some other way of doing it?' Guthrie again.

'I don't really see why, Jonathan.'

'Because people will say, your audiences will say, "There you
are, Olivier all over."'

'Yes?'

'If you want to stamp yourself vocally all over the role, just
be Olivier being Olivier, then go ahead. You don't need me for
that.'

Slowly he made me see myself as others saw me. He wanted
to help me out of it; I'd made a mountain out of mannerisms and
had ended up impersonating myself. It's a habit that old actors
fall for very easily. Miller opened my eyes and made me look in
the mirror again.

It was a good lesson to learn, and one so easy to miss. As in
every business, once you have become a success people are
more inclined to be sycophantic, everything you do is perfect –
it must be, you are the leader. If you are wrong then a whole
dynasty collapses; therefore you must be right. Any criticisms,
any rumblings of dissent, are made some way off, out of hearing.
This doesn't happen so much in the theatre as it does in other
businesses; in the theatre there is much more equality, in a way
you are only as good as your last job. Mind you, having said
that, perhaps I'm wrong: maybe it does happen as often in the
theatre, perhaps it was happening to me and I just went merrily
along thinking I was right and must be right because nobody told
me I was wrong.

I'm not saying that what I had done in my early days at the
National had fallen into Olivier doing Olivier – far from it – I'm
saying that when I started the rehearsals for *The Merchant* I had
obviously slipped into this error; Jonathan spotted it and had the
courage to point it out.

By the time I had reached the National I was not only the

leading actor but also manager of the whole set-up as well. I had very fine associate directors, but, when it came down to it, I was the boss. I was approaching sixty and had been at the top of my profession for some years, so it couldn't have been easy for people to summon up the courage to tell me I was wrong. They did, of course, in administration, but when it came to the acting I was the 'Guv'nor'. Naturally there were arguments about the choice of plays and, indeed, as I have said in my other book, the scales did not always come down in my favour. But when it came to acting, I knew best and, if I didn't, it wasn't for them to tell me. This sounds arrogant and I suppose it is; what I'm really trying to say is that my ear was open, but no one chose to whisper into it until Jonathan Miller did.

Inevitably old actors do repeat themselves. It's so easy. If it worked before, it will work again. I don't think I consciously thought in this way; in fact, I didn't. If I had, I'd have stopped it right away myself. No, it was definitely in the subconscious. I suppose, when a little tiredness creeps into the bones, some aid from the past doesn't go amiss. I had been well known for my inflections over the years, the changing of pace, and the sudden surges of power, so why not pluck a few moments from my past?

But, as I say, it came as a bit of a shock when Jonathan pointed the finger. For a moment I returned to school, my satchel full of embarrassment. Here was I, the one actor who had always prided himself on his originality, and here was a young director telling me I was as original as yesterday's newspaper. For a moment my mind flashed around some of my contemporaries. I paused. 'He's right,' I thought – a deep breath – 'He's right.' And I trust that from that moment I stopped living in my own image and began afresh.

I had seen George Arliss play Disraeli in a 1929 movie, and it suggested shades of the Shylock that I wanted to give. So again, without embarrassment, I must acknowledge another actor. You must remember that when I say I've used other performers to unlock the gates for me in certain roles, it is always my interpretation in the end. I am not a mimic, I am a purveyor of plays.

So the process began again, the process of moulding and building, and becoming a character. I studied and watched in trains, buses, streets, taxis. I observed the populace. Soon I became aware that the so-called Jewish nose was to be seen more frequently on Gentile faces than on Jewish ones. This pleased me because, as I have already said, this was not the way I wanted to play it. Then suddenly I saw what it was: the mouth, it was the mouth that was different. Larger, much more sensitive, much more mobile. A visit to the dentist was necessary.

I had teeth made that totally altered the shape of my face. They pulled my mouth out and pushed my upper lip forward. Suddenly there he was, my Shylock. Months of sitting and staring at noses that didn't exist, and there it was all the time. The mouth was the thing. The moment I saw it in the mirror I knew I was right.

It was a lesson well learnt. Don't look for the obvious. If anything, that's usually the caricature; go the other way, be more subtle in your choice. Look for the mole, the tic, the wart, the walk, the handshake, the smile. Mouths are very interesting and can be altered so easily. By doing this you can completely reshape a face and create a character. Thin lips, fat lips, crooked lips, hare lips and so on. Just look how much a moustache changes a face; change the moustache and again the character changes. What has happened to the actor's face between entering the dressing room and coming out again tells the story. Try whitening the face as an experiment. Reduce your face to nothing with a white pancake, and then add one thing and see what you make of it. Dab a spot on and see what it does. Take it away again and add an eyebrow, take the eyebrow away and add a moustache, and so on. Very interesting what you may discover. For instance, have you ever thought of playing a character who has just shaved his moustache off? That feeling of nakedness on the upper lip: the fingers flick to it frequently to see if it really has gone. Nobody of course in the play will refer to it, but it will add something to your performance which might just give it an extra depth, a little more colour, just a little different.

There are a million things that you can add to the make-up of your mind. And these are the things that will eventually make your character exist. I'm not suggesting that an actor go over the top; that would only be deeply irritating to the audience and your fellow actors alike. But experiment and see what you find. The mouth and eyes are all-important.

So I had my new teeth and immediately I felt right. My only concern was that Jonathan Miller might take one look and confiscate them. But I think he was so relieved that I hadn't put on a false nose, he willingly let me keep them.

Part of my Shylock was based on an uncle of mine, the first Lord Olivier – I am the second. Uncle Sydney was part of the first Labour Government of 1924: he was Secretary of State for India. He was a remarkable man. He was twice Governor of Jamaica, which was quite a feat, to have two innings at the one job as it were. He was obviously very popular and well liked.

I remember he came to stay once, and father had spent the few household pennies on vintage port and good food. Uncle Sydney was to have the best. He had a beard and looked quite Jewish, which in his early days created a slight problem, for in spite of Disraeli's success, it still made life difficult for politicians.

There was a dignity and bearing about Uncle Sydney that was an enormous help in my search for Shylock. I remembered it and used it.

My performance remained contained in uprightness and civility until Jessica was stolen away, and then, with justification, slowly went demented. To take the daughter was like carving the heart out of Shylock, and this I tried to emphasize in the role. The departure of his daughter turned his brain. Once this happened, he was prepared to sue, to destroy. Once she had gone off with a Gentile, as far as he was concerned she was dead. The pound of flesh was nothing compared with the abduction. He had been raped by a pack of Christian dogs. From that moment onwards I let the fury and the rages come.

It was during the run of *The Merchant* that I suffered badly from the actor's nightmare – *stage fright*. I wonder if that had anything to do with my performance becoming fresh, open and naked again? It's always possible.

Let me give you a brief insight into stage fright. It comes in all sorts of forms; I suppose it's always there, but most of the time it hovers unseen. It is an animal, a monster which hides in its foul corner without revealing itself, but you know that it is there and that it may come forward at any moment. A shadow in a lightless room, it's lurking there in the back of your brain cells, an insubstantial presence that refuses to go away. At any moment it will push a finger forward and knock over the 'operator' who is waiting at your 'exchange' for the next message to be received, translated and sent to another part of your body. The next message can't get through. Stage fright is like the character in *The Turn of the Screw* who never appears: he is always waiting outside the door, any door, waiting to get you. You either battle or walk away.

For people who haven't had it it is very difficult to understand. To the young actor who is full of optimism and energy it is a joke. I'm certain I didn't believe in it when I was young and hopeful. I don't suppose I even gave it a thought. But suddenly there he is: the bogeyman comes along and tries to rob you of your living. He can come at any time, in any form. The dark shadow of fear.

Sometimes the process can begin in bed at night, the night before a performance. Hot and cold sweats suddenly wake you, your brain leaps into top gear, thinking of the performance to come. The logical fighting the illogical.

I don't know the lines, dear God, I don't know the lines.

Of course you do. You know them backwards.

That's not the point. I don't want to know them backwards. I just want to know them.

You know them. You know you know them.

Let me just go through them again.

What's the point? Sleep, you really must sleep.

To hell with sleep. I'll go through the whole blasted script, that's what I'll do. I'll go through the whole thing.

It's pointless.

I'll write it all out in longhand. I'll go through it syllable by syllable.

How like a fawning publican he looks!
I hate him for he is a Christian . . .

Next, what's next? For God's sake, what comes next?
Relax.
I'll get up . . . I'll get up and walk round the house. I'll recite
the whole play out loud until it is so bored with me, it will reside
in my memory box forever.
And up I'd get, the hot sweat having turned to cold.
Panic . . . that's all it is. People get like this in the early hours
of the morning . . . it's a well-known fact.
Come on back to bed . . . you'll feel better in the morning.
Maybe you're right . . . maybe. I'm really very tired . . . I
need to sleep.
Back to bed, feeling cold now, blankets pulled up round the
ears. Sleeping in fits and starts. Sudden moments of wide
awakeness, and other moments of deep sleep. Night-
mares . . . black holes . . . bright colours . . . suddenly it's
morning.
As I have said, it comes in many forms, creeps up and swamps
you like a shadow, and just when you think you've conquered
it, there it is sitting at the end of the bed grinning at you.
There is the kind of stage fright that begins when you are
waiting in the wings and you can hear your cue approaching.
The heart starts to pound and you can feel it at the base of your
spine. It is nothing like first-night nerves, it is way beyond that.
The breathing becomes affected, the breath becomes shorter
when you want to make it longer and deeper, and all the time
this wretched cue is getting nearer. You try to calm down but
the sweat breaks out again. The voice in the head starts to
ramble.
I should have stayed in the dressing room . . . why do I
subject myself to this? I've done it all . . . I've done everything
. . . why don't I stop now while I'm on top?
The cue is getting nearer.
I'm not going to be able to go on . . . I'm rooted to the spot.
Somebody has nailed my shoes to the floor. My legs are made

of lead. I'm alone, oh God, how alone I am. Nobody understands
this . . . nobody.

Cue nearly here.

I'm going to walk out into that bright glare and be utterly
exposed. Walk out? Nonsense. I can't leave here. I'll never
move again. I'm going to be rooted to this spot for ever.

PORTIA. . . . *If he have the condition of a saint and the complexion
of a devil . . .*

If I don't go on now I'll never go on again.

PORTIA. . . . *I had rather he should shrive me than wive me . . .*

This is the theatre where I have played Hamlet, Richard,
Henry . . . This is my theatre . . . my beloved theatre. This
can't happen here . . . I will not let it happen here . . . I am in
control . . . I have got to be in control . . . I am . . . I am . . .

PORTIA. . . . *Come Nerissa. Sirrah, go before. Whiles we shut the
gate upon one wooer, another knocks at the door.*

Now . . . that's it . . . now. The next lines to be spoken are
mine. Move . . . Move . . .

The thumping at the base of the spine is now almost painful.
This is what it must be like to give birth.

I go forward. Slowly I go forward.

Shylock . . . you're Shylock. Am I? Am I really? I'm not . . .
I'm just me . . . stage-frightened me.

Suddenly I'm there. The wing is left behind and I'm on.

I have given instructions to the other actors not to look me
in the eyes. My company, what a thing to do to them. But I had
to. The one thing an actor must do is look his fellow actor in the
eyes and I have asked my fellow players not to.

SHYLOCK. *Three thousand ducats; well?*

I've said it . . . the line's out. I've said the first line. God, supposing I fall over. I've got the feeling I'm going to fall over.

BASSANIO. *Ay, sir, for three months.*

I mustn't fall over.

SHYLOCK. *For three months; well?*

Second line out . . . I've said two lines. Why can't I get rid of this lack of balance? Lack of sense of balance.

BASSANIO. *For the which, as I told you, Antonio shall be bound.*

Relax . . . that's all I've got to do . . . relax.

SHYLOCK. *Antonio shall be bound . . . well.*

What happens if I fall over now? Balance . . . come on balance.

BASSANIO. *May you stead me? Will you pleasure me? Shall I know your answer?*

The lines are echoing. I'm in an echo chamber . . . 'Shall I know your answer?' What is my answer? Calm, stay calm. My heart is racing. Speak . . . it's your turn. What is it? What do I say? I know it . . . I know the line . . . what is it . . . what is it? Come on . . . come on . . . I've been here for an hour . . . I've paused for an hour. Why aren't they coughing? Anything . . . just say anything . . .

SHYLOCK. *Three thousand ducats, for three months, and Antonio bound.*

I've done it . . . that's the right line. I've done it.

Once you have experienced stage fright, you are always aware that it could be just around the corner waiting for you, just waiting for you to get cocky and over-confident. So you treat the body and the brain with much more respect, and you always remain conscious of the shadow in the corner.

I find the play horrid and cruel, and none of the characters likeable. Shylock is just better-quality stuff than any of the Christians in the play, who are heartless, money-grubbing monsters. But I have much to thank the play for. It finally put down my stage fright. Now I can say, 'I have been there, I have looked over the edge, and I have returned.'

People have asked me about the cry that I let out off stage when Shylock exited after the court scene, mortified by the judgement. I wanted something to remain ringing in the ears long after I was in the dressing room. Something that would stay with the audience through the sweetness and light of the final romantic comic scene.

I used to leave and deliberately lose my footing in the wings. I'd fall forwards and smash the palms of my hands on the concrete floor. Then the real pain would make me cry and sob like a child. A dramatic way of doing it maybe, but an effective one. There he was, his dignity gone, a case lost, because he was a Jew. The trip off stage drove him into infuriated grief.

Many of the great actors of the past had finished the play on Shylock's final exit: Kean for one. I didn't, and wouldn't even if it had been suggested. Shakespeare wrote the play to finish in Belmont, and finish in Belmont it should. But Shylock should remain. Beneath the humour there should be a sad shadow of a destroyed man. For me the cry did it.

PART THREE

CONTEMPORARY
INFLUENCES

ELEVEN

KNIGHTS OF THE THEATRE

I've known Ralph Richardson and John Gielgud for many, many years and we've acted together on innumerable occasions, lately more often on the screen. Hollywood would send for us, the three knights, in the hopes that our names would assist the mogul's box-office receipts. I don't know that it ever did, but I suppose it might have done.

You can hear them in their high-rise Californian offices now, can't you? 'What we need is a bit of class . . . get me one of them Limey guys with a handle to his name . . . better still, get me three.' And there we'd be, the threesome: Ralph, John and Larry. I'm not knocking it, believe me; there were times when it was very useful. Even now I can look at an acre of land with satisfaction and say to myself, 'Ah, such and such bought that . . .'

It's difficult to talk about contemporaries. I don't know why I am doing it, really. What I should be doing is talking about how it was done, not who it was done with or what others were doing at the same time. Yet it is difficult to avoid it. We actors beg to be adored, appreciated, admired, so we must every now and then be allowed to be discovered with our trousers down. There are always going to be tales about actors that will amuse or shock their public – usually apocryphal, but fun. We all have skeletons in our wardrobes. The actor quite deliberately sets himself up for this kind of treatment; we are the Aunt Sallies of the world!

Looking back, I suppose we all took ourselves rather seriously: when we let the humour and the vulnerability creep in, we get much closer to the truth. This was especially true of John Gielgud in his early days. Now that he appears to regard himself with a sense of humour he has become a much finer actor. Once he threw off the finery and took an honest look at himself in the glass, his acting became much richer and more truthful. His performances in *Home* and *No Man's Land*, for instance, showed him at his stunning best. He is a character actor and it is good to see he's got holes in his socks. He has a delicious sense of humour and at last he is letting it grin through. He no longer needs the sticks of five-and-nine make-up and the voice that wooed the world.

I remember when we worked together in that early production of *Romeo and Juliet*, how I was the whipping boy and John was the adored god. At that time John was the king of the West End, he was already a huge star and quite rightly enjoyed it. I don't say that with any envy, for indeed I was a star as well, but I was still considered a movie actor. I was more of an upstart, I suppose – in the eyes of the Establishment, that is, not in my own eyes, certainly not in my own. I have always had that rod of steel in my make-up; flexible, but there. I have always very much believed in myself, as of course every actor must.

John is a very sweet man, but he seems to say rather more critical things about me than he does about Ralph. He probably wouldn't agree with this, and I've more than likely got it all wrong; I mean I'm sure he's fond of me really, but somehow something still niggles in the back of my mind. He harks back every now and again to how terrible he thought I was as Romeo; but that was over forty-five years ago. Surely you don't have to harbour unpleasant thoughts about people for forty-five years? I know that my Romeo, to say the least, was controversial, but it was also ultimately a success. At the time, of course, opinion was very much out of my favour. I was a slightly bigger success than John as Mercutio, but he made a vastly bigger success than I did as Romeo, and that hurt because Romeo was what I saw myself as. The theatrical world had not yet reached the 'Wouldn't it be fun if it were a bit more real?' idea. Never mind about

'Wouldn't it be more fun . . . ?' We should have been asking ourselves, 'Wouldn't it be right to find reality?' For it is not a game of charades, this acting world of ours; it is an everlasting search for the truth. We must never allow ourselves to be blinkered by sighs from the wings. We must guard our talents from false adulation. We must insist on holding a piece of rock in our palms and not brightly-coloured plastic.

We were, and indeed are, very different actors and people. I will always be an active actor, and John a passive one. I'm a peripheral player who goes out to the character, whereas he stays in the centre, finds something in the part that will suit him, then pulls it in towards himself. I went for the physical, the heroics if you like, whereas John was always the poet, the ephemerist, head upturned towards the stars. I always appeared to be firmly astride this earth, eyes level on the horizon. Two very different actors, both with one thing in mind: success. I don't think I'd have wanted to play Richard II, and I don't think John was moulded to play Richard III. It might have been fascinating if we had; but only for us, a collector's item. Mind you, I'd have given him a merry ride as Bolingbroke.

John has a dignity, a majesty which suggests that he was born with a crown on his head; on the other hand my persona is that of a man who has plucked the crown up and placed it on himself. I am Bosworth Field and Agincourt; and John is Pomfret Castle.

Today, for me, John has somehow completed the acting circle. He has found his centre, he is a brilliant character actor. The pain behind the glasses in *No Man's Land* was electrifying . . . the bare soul covered with a thin veneer of sophistication. You could see the clouds passing across his face like a day in an English acre. The sun popping out on the odd moment giving a façade of warmth and happiness . . . not a summer sun, a winter sun. That performance created a reality that I've always fought for.

Ralph was one of the finest actors of this century; pound for pound he could take on anyone in the theatrical ring. He was brilliant, and I think would have stood shoulder high in any century. Come to that, I think, pound for pound, he could have taken on anyone in the boxing ring. He had amazing strength

and poetic gentleness. He could play gods and common men
with equal majesty. I loved him dearly and find it very difficult
to believe that he has gone. Somehow I always expect to find
him in the next room or round the next corner, or to hear him
screaming up the back lane on his beloved motorbike. He was
larger than life but, at the same time, was able to present life
with complete clarity and truth. He could take a line and twist
it and make it remain in your head for ever. He had wonderful,
generous features – God! what an actor's face. Broad, bold and
easy to read. A fine, incredible man and a most dear friend. We
laughed together, dreamed together, drank together, worked
and played together. We were rivals in the best sense of the
word and, for a time, we ran a theatre together, which I think
during that period was the best around. Peer Gynt, Richard III,
Cyrano, Henry V, Falstaff – we were pretty special. I learned a
lot from him, our friendship going back as far as Barry Jackson
and Birmingham days. I suppose, in a way, I was a bit like Hal
to his Falstaff. He was an established actor in the company when
I joined, so we all looked up to him with a great deal of respect.
He was the leading man.

Ralph was equally at home in comedy or tragedy: he wore
the mask of both. He could take you from a moment of high
comedy into deep tragedy with a nod. The audience loved him,
and the camera treated him with the adulation of a young lover.
It adored him, and he seemed to adore it. He moulded it round
his performances like warm putty; it was as though it had been
invented just for him. I can see him now on the cliffs watching
the seagulls in *The Sound Barrier*, or standing by the fireplace
in *The Heiress*, the camera seeming to fit round him like an old
and deeply loved armchair. He even smoked a pipe as though
he'd invented it. I only have to think of him for a moment and I
can hear his voice. He was warm and what the public might call
ordinary and, therefore, quite exceptional. That was his ability,
that was his talent; he really was a man for all seasons.

When the theatre set off on its new path, led by George
Devine and the new young directors and actors, he took it all
with ease in his great, giant steps and, after a time, you began
to feel that he had changed the course of the theatre entirely on

his own. His performance in Pinter's *No Man's Land* and Storey's *Home* were classics on their own. Finely-tuned moments of theatrical magic. He could at times hold an audience in the palm of his hand and bend down and whisper an earful of delights. He could take you through *Peer Gynt* and make hours seem like seconds, with a wry brain and an eyeful of smiles. He was a conjurer, a magician. He was Everyman with a touch of – dare I say it – genius. He spoke poetry with the air of someone who had just written it, and made you feel you were hearing it for the first time. Of course, he was always aware of the verse, but this was his cunning: he made you feel that it was taking care of itself. His voice had such clarity, he chose his words with great care and placed them where others would fear to tread. He had the ability to make it look easy, always the sign of a great artist. With Ralph it all looked so simple. I often got the impression that his audience wanted to be up there with him, the whole process looked so enjoyable. He could make believe better than most. I always used to think he was on another planet.

I remember his first entrance in R. C. Sherriff's *Home at Seven*, a play about a businessman who has gone missing for twenty-four hours, during which time a murder has been committed. He brought the complete character on stage with what appeared to be no effort at all. You sat there and thought, 'This *is* the man.' He didn't have to speak, he *was* David Preston, the perfect city businessman. You could see him on the morning commuter train with *The Times* rolled under his arm, the furled umbrella and the bowler hat. You knew what his desk at the office was like, you knew how he drank his tea.

Ralph was a great after-dinner speaker; he seemed to be a natural. Give him the opportunity and he'd stay there all night. He had enormous wit, and his timing was as accurate as Big Ben. I think perhaps he would have made a great comic in the music halls. He throve on his audience. When Ralph was on the bill at a charity concert or a memorial you always added ten minutes to your original timing; once his anecdotes started, he couldn't stop. Not that anybody wanted him to; they were only too happy to sit at his feet and be mesmerized by his charm.

The most amazing and outrageous things would happen to
Ralph. I'm sure he wouldn't mind me telling you the story of his
two visits to two houses we once had. He's probably told the
story himself countless times, and much better than I can place
it on these pages, but I'll tell you all the same.

The first house was a darling place called Durham Cottage,
which Vivien and I were very proud of. He came down for dinner
with his divine wife, Meriel Forbes, known to us all as Mu, a
wonderful lady. The three of us, Vivien, Mu and myself, were
very much aware of dear Ralph's taste in wines – a pretty poor
one at the best of times – and we had a priceless bottle of
burgundy which we intended to consume without the assistance
of the merry monarch. So, what I did was place a bottle of
champagne in front of him and say, 'There you are, Ralph, that's
yours. As soon as that's finished, there's loads more. You don't
have to stop drinking because you've come to the end of the
bottle. When you've finished that one, just get tucked into the
next.' His eyes twinkled and everything seemed settled. The
three of us wine fanciers got stuck into our burgundy and purred
a lot. All was right with our world.

The trouble was that Ralph took me seriously and didn't stop
when he had consumed the first bottle; consequently he got
gloriously stewed. Everything would have been fine, except for
one thing. It was Vivien's birthday, 5 November, Guy Fawkes'
Day, and, as a treat, Ralph had brought some fireworks, which
he always loved.

We had not been in the house very long and everything was
absolutely perfect as far as we were concerned: freshly painted
and pristine, newly furnished and looking, as we thought, impec-
cable. Even the outside was looking splendid. The garden had
just been started, there was a little pond with a statue fountain
and the right things planted round it. I've always been in love
with gardens.

Suddenly, at the table, Ralph sat bolt upright and exclaimed:
'Fireworks.'

I panicked.

There was a pause, he grinned at me and then stood. 'Fireworks.'

I attempted a smile, the burgundy turning to acid, and enquired, 'Fireworks?'

He winked. 'It's Vivien's birthday and Guy Fawkes' joy day, can't let that go without a bang or two, can we?'

I knew I was beaten. 'Ralph, how sweet you are, what a lovely thought.'

'Right,' he said.

I jumped in: 'Outside, Ralph, all right? They'll be fine outside. This is all so new and we're proud of it. The ladies can watch from the window.'

'Oh my dear fellow,' he said, and started to laugh. He gave my face a playful slap – he always slapped one's face much too hard. I thought, 'Here we go, I've had it, there's nothing I can do.' And so he started. He began by letting off squibs from the dining-room window sill and, of course, scarred it with huge burns. He then nailed a Catherine wheel to a beautiful weeping cotoneaster and I could see the poor tree dying before my eyes. He stuck them on the mantelpiece, he stuck them on the walnut bureau, he stuck them everywhere.

After a time my anger began to come to the surface and, despite his absolutely bemused state, he began to sense my disapproval. He suddenly stopped and looked around at us all. He paused for a moment and then grabbed Mu's hand and said, 'Come on Mu, best leave these people', and burst through the French windows, shattering the lock and a couple of panes of glass. Once in the garden, he really hit the heights. From the French windows he found the pond, stepped into it, knocking the statue over, then stepped out again, leaving a dead goldfish or two in his wake. Then he proceeded to move on down the garden. He passed through a hedge of lilac that I had just planted, a bumbling, grumbling bear, and then on to the front gate, which he pushed through, slammed shut, and the handle fell off. He then disappeared into the night.

It really was very funny; there's no way it could have been staged with such perfection. Every gag was used in what might have been the original hasty exit. Dear Ralph.

The next time he paid a visit we had moved from Durham Cottage to an even more splendid place, Notley Abbey. Notley was near Thame, halfway between Stratford and London, and was very, very beautiful. Of all the houses I've lived in over the years, Notley is my favourite. It was absolutely enchanting, and enchanted me. At Notley I had an affair with the past. For me it had mesmeric power; I could easily drown in its atmosphere. I could not leave it alone, I was a child lost in its history. Perhaps I loved it too much, if that is possible.

It had been built by Walter Giffard, Earl of Buckingham, during the reign of Henry II, 'in order that the souls of the King, his Queen Eleanor of Aquitaine, his own soul and those of all his family, might be prayed for in perpetuity'. Whenever I returned to Notley after a period away, I felt safe and secure. I had my castle.

When Ralph came down he was truly on his best behaviour after Durham Cottage, and it seemed he was determined to be the most enthusiastic guest we'd ever had. He insisted on seeing everything.

'My dear Laurence, you must show me everything. You must take me from top to bottom and show me every single detail. I insist.'

'Right,' I said, 'let's start with the frescos and the ceiling of the part of it that was the Great Hall.' And off we went.

The hall was filled with Latin quotations all going round and round. A dado of Latin quotations. There were very pretty colours and some of the walls had tiny violets stencilled onto them. I knew this would be a favourite haunt of mine, somewhere I'd always like to show people if they were remotely interested in the period. It was fascinating.

To get there I used to go up the tower and then across one room which had been turned into a sort of box room, and then along a bit where I'd floored just a sort of passageway and nothing else, so you can imagine it was a trifle precarious.

Ralph would stop every few minutes to admire something deeply. 'Oh, it's beautiful. Oh, Laurence, what a marvellously fortunate fellow you are. Oh, isn't it beautiful', and so on. We stopped at one point on the passageway that I'd floored, and Ralph looked at something in particular – can't think what it was now. He looked for some time, scrutinizing every detail, playing the part of the Historian; any moment, I thought, he's going to produce a magnifying glass. After a pause, he said, 'Oh, my dear fellow, the wonder of it, oh the beauty . . .' At this moment, bound in the cocoon of his absolute rapturous pleasure, he stepped off my carefully laid passageway and went straight through the ceiling into the spare bedroom below.

What a man! I adored him.

Over the years I often asked him for advice, and he was always very much to the point.

'Ralph . . .'

'Hullo, dear boy, how are you?'

'Ralph, shall I go to the Old Vic?'

'Think it's a very good idea.'

'Thanks. Goodbye.'

My Richard III had been an enormous success at the Old Vic with, as I have already mentioned, *Peer Gynt* and *Arms and the Man*. Naturally, after their successes, Europe and America beckoned. We were asked to perform all three in Paris and New York.

Ralph had played the first night and the last of the season at the Vic, with *Peer Gynt,* and I felt that it was now my turn to kick off on the tour, and so I put it to him that I should go first.

'Old cock, I'm sorry . . . but you played . . . you took the first night of all and the last night of the first season with your play. Now, in Europe, it's my turn. I'll be the first, if you don't mind.'

Poor fellow had to agree. I knew full well that the first off in Paris, or wherever we played in Europe, would be the big one in the critics' estimation. They'd recognize that that was top. I knew what I was doing all right. So, when the season closed in London, we set off for Paris with the 'sweet smell' still in our nostrils.

We opened, and *Richard III* was an outstanding success. After the cheers and the wining and dining, I returned to the hotel, treasuring my triumph and thinking what a clever fellow I was to go first. I was sitting in my hotel room at a desk by the window, writing a letter to Vivien, full of my first-night glory, when a strange thing happened that I never really got to the bottom of. I hadn't seen much of Ralph after the show; he'd obviously headed off to do his thing, as I had mine.

I'd got to a part of the letter, which read 'I'm worried Ralph has . . .', when I suddenly heard this noise on the pipes outside. I went to the window and looked out. There, below me, I could see a figure attempting to climb up the drainpipes in my direction. On closer inspection I saw that it was a dishevelled, inebriated Ralph.

'Ralph,' I yelled, 'do you want to kill yourself?'

At first he didn't seem to hear me, so determined was he.

'Get down, Ralph, get down.'

He suddenly looked up towards me, paused for a moment, hesitated, *grinned*, and returned to the earth. He disappeared and I went downstairs to let him in. Before I could ask him where he'd been, what had happened, what was the problem, he pushed me roughly aside and walked up the stairs.

'Get out of my way,' he mumbled. Perhaps he thought I was in *his* room, I don't know.

We'd had sort of friendly quarrels before, but they were always all right. Perhaps a little deadliness behind them, no more. We'd always had a jealousy, a rivalry, about what we could do and what we could not do. We were for ever trying to outgun each other, which was healthy and good for business; but somehow this night there seemed to be something more involved.

He stood still for a moment, then suddenly lunged towards me and picked me up in his arms like a baby. Within strides, he had crossed the room and was on to the balcony. I thought, 'It'll stop now, the joke's over.' But it wasn't. He moved with me in his arms across the balcony and held me over the edge. I couldn't believe it was happening. Here I was, a fully-grown man, not without strength of my own, being held like a child by my best friend above a Parisian street.

When you know there is nothing between you and the hard cobbles sixty feet below, except a pair of strong arms, time really does stand still. I knew that if I struggled, he would let me go, and so I remained as still and as calm as I possibly could, which isn't easy when your heart is running at a hundred miles a minute. Supposing he slipped? Supposing he got tired? Oh hell! It is true, everything does rush before you. What a way to go, half way through a letter to Vivien . . .

Very quietly I spoke. 'Ralph . . . I think we'll all look very silly in the morning.'

Pause. Nothing.

'Why don't you pull me back?'

Still nothing. In the silence I could feel him breathing.

'Look . . . why don't you pull me back like a good boy? I'm beginning to feel really nervous.'

Another pause. Then slowly he brought me back in. He put me on my feet inside the balcony and we both stood there looking at each other. I saw in his eyes that if I'd done anything other than I had, he'd have let me go. For a brief moment he'd wanted to kill me.

We moved back into the warm room. I closed the balcony windows behind me. It was wonderful to smell the stuffy, centrally-heated air instead of the cold Parisian night.

I said, as casually as I could, 'That was a rather dangerous one, wasn't it, Ralph?' He admitted that it was, then quietly left and went to his own room. I just sat there, not being able to believe what had happened.

The next morning we sat together at breakfast. Over the coffee I repeated, 'Ralph, that was rather a near one, wasn't it?'

He said 'Yeah.' He bit a piece of toast and then continued, 'Yes, we were both very foolish. It was a double fault.'

I couldn't believe what I was hearing . . . a double fault! He held me over a balcony and threatened to drop me, threatened to spread my life all over the pavement and it was *my* doing? There are some thrills you can do without.

What a man! Looking back, I laugh sometimes to think what the consequences might have been. If he'd dropped me, I'd have been acting with Henry Irving much sooner than I'd anticipated, and a short time afterwards Ralph would have joined me, having done a brief dance on the end of a rope. There would have been no more Old Vic as far as we were concerned. But then maybe that wouldn't have displeased some people.

Whatever else, he was a great man. I treasured him dearly,

and he will be with me forever. They were golden days, and we were the golden boys, blessed with God's sunshine.

Watching John and Ralph spark off each other over the past few years on stage and on screen has been a real joy: the contrasts rich in flavour, like eating a good meal, looking at a fine painting, or listening to Mozart. They were so in tune, though able to descant to each other at will, like a brilliant double act. That wicked glimpse from Ralph at the audience saying, 'This is my turn, look at me', and then John gently steering the eyes back in his direction, with complete authority.

They were in such charge of their acting machinery, would that they could have gone on forever, but now sadly the elder of the party has gone and the two-man band has been reduced to a single turn again.

It was a dream to watch them, all guns blazing, and we must be grateful to the inspired managements who had the insight to put them together.

TWELVE

BREAKTHROUGH

I talked of timing earlier and I think it is important, not just in acting but also in life itself. I have somehow always had a nose for the way fashion might go; I have always attempted to be there at the precise time the old order changeth, whether it be for the better or not. That is why, I think, I have managed to remain an accounted success for most of my life. I have continually sniffed the theatrical air searching for the winds of change.

When I first saw *Look Back in Anger*, I didn't really take to it at all. 'Angry Young Man'. So what? A new term coined by journalists to sell newspapers . . . And yet, at the same time I did sense something was happening. I felt that this might well be one of the theatre's great turning points. It wasn't the play itself so much as its articulateness, the new sense of drama it projected. The theatre seemed to have a new message and, if so, this message must be respected.

Sometimes you'll find yourself somewhere by chance or by mistake, and your awareness, for some reason unknown to you, becomes doubly acute. A badly-lit alley, and halfway along instinct tells you this is dangerous. Do you go on and out into the blind side, or do you retreat and return to the place you know? You cannot flip a coin, you must make a firm decision: the middle is mugger's paradise, you must either skulk back or leap on. I know what I do. It's because of this that I've been able to enjoy my working life for so many years. It has been magical, and I wouldn't have had it any other way. Let's face it, it's much better than going to the office.

I think I am what I might term an immediate man, always ready for the next second of life. Someone once asked me, 'What's it like to know that you will live long after you're dead?'

I replied, 'Where's the glamour in that? Westminster Abbey is just as cold as any village graveyard. Nobody wants to die.'

Using that immediacy, I have always been prepared to turn on a sixpence, like a boxer reading the eyes of the opposition. Guard always up and, if hit, never show it. Smile.

It was suggested that I should see *Look Back in Anger* again, which I did. It was on this second occasion that I became certain that Mother Theatre had given birth to a monster who was spitting, clawing and elbowing its way through the tradition that the previous generation had built and settled for. The child was transforming everything, and almost overnight. It was out of nappies before most of my generation was aware that it was born. Not only was it out of nappies, it was here to stay and would have an effect on acting as well as on plays being written.

Of course I do not perform as a new young actor does. If the new generation were required to do what I do now, they would have extreme difficulty, because it took a long time to arrive at where I am. But I feel that if they were to teach me their job, they would find that I could grasp it quite quickly, because I'm well versed in my work.

I went backstage afterwards and, having exchanged the usual formal compliments, I was introduced to the man himself. 'Larry, this is John Osborne . . .'

The writer is the recorder of our times, the actor the interpreter, and it is the producer's job to fuse them. In this case, George Devine.

Working with Devine at the Royal Court, I was forced to reassess my ideas. It changed my acting career just when it needed a shot in the arm. My career was becoming predictable, solid and rather dull, but Devine changed all that. I felt that to the youth at the Royal Court, as my wife Joan later corroborated, I seemed Establishment, and probably set in my theatrical ways.

Very understandable. I was aware that Vivien and I had been known as the Royal Couple of British Theatre.

I was not the 'king' about to bless the people from my throne of talent, I was a worker like everybody else. A man of other people's letters. So I didn't need much encouragement from George Devine. I knew where I was going. I took the banner of my generation to them. I was in there long before John Gielgud or Ralph Richardson knew it existed. I said to John Osborne, 'God, I wish you'd write a play for me one day.'

The first act of *The Entertainer* was sent to me in New York. I read it straight away and decided that the part of Billy Rice, the old father, was for me. I found him fascinating. You could feel the music hall in his old bones, and I believed I could do something rather special with him.

I called George in London and told him I was interested, and I imagine he conveyed my interest to John Osborne. I heard John quoted later on as saying that he never writes with any particular actor in mind. Maybe this is so; I cannot argue with what he claims to be true. All I can say is that, when the rest of *The Entertainer* arrived in New York, nobody was going to play the part of Archie but me.

Billy was a good part, a magnificent part, but when I read the completed script, Archie leapt off the page at me and he had to be mine. I called George immediately and told him that *The Entertainer* would be my next project.

Almost at once I began to steep myself in the old music-hall tradition. It wasn't too difficult because it was there in John's play – that, and so many other things. The play was enormous, a huge canvas. The winds of change were there all right. I was in step with the new wave, in step and marching. The recorder, the interpreter and the producer.

What an amazing man George Devine was. I felt he was my closest friend. He had tremendous vision and insight. When you look back and see what happened at the Royal Court in Sloane Square in the 1950s, you cannot fail to be astonished at the achievements. What a sad and premature loss his death was.

So the 'king' came to the Court, not the Court to the 'king'.

The play had been written with superb technique . . . that

wonderful scene about the cake, Phoebe's sense of violation when she finds a piece of the cake has been cut. However, I had a problem with the telling of rotten jokes because it was very hard not to win the audience over too soon. To begin with they were charmed and amused by my sallies, captivated by my virtuosity; but gradually I had to build on the sense of sadness, tiredness and threadbareness until there wasn't a laugh anywhere in the house. Then I knew, well, that's come off. However, it was no good struggling to put them against me with the first one, no good at all. I had to be extremely slow to reveal what an unsympathetic character I really was.

I will always be grateful for those days and look back on them with affection. Archie Rice: there he stands in the bright spotlight, alone, laughless but smiling. A bowler hat, a cane, eyebrows, a gap in his teeth, and dead eyes . . .

I suppose wherever I go there will always be a piece of Sloane Square in my heart.

I talk as though the Royal Court was new to me. This is not exactly true; I had played there twenty-nine years before. But what it represented in 1957 was very new to me. I had appeared there in 1928 with the Birmingham Repertory Company, from January to May, playing Malcolm in a modern-dress *Macbeth*, the title role in *Harold* (Tennyson), the Lord in *The Taming of the Shrew* (offered me palpably to check if I'd got a swollen head) and the Young Man in *The Adding Machine* (Elmer Rice). Strange that I should have returned as *Archie* Rice.

Archie, the song-and-dance man reduced to appearing twice nightly in nude revue, lecherous, corrupt and blue with a talent for destructive self-analysis. I always saw him as an intelligent man aware of his failure, pushing it under the carpet under a haze of gin. He knew where he was and what he'd become, and the only way to cope with it was to abdicate all responsibility. I thought John Osborne had put the whole of contemporary England on stage with one amazing sweep of his brush. It was an epic painting and the strokes were brilliantly bold.

I have always found the music hall fascinating. Such courage, such bravura, the painted smile on the comic's face when the house is laughterless and all the mackintoshes want are the stationary nudes. There's theatre for you. The broken heart that floats in a sea of gin. The staring eyes with nothing behind them. Clowns have always made me want to cry.

The music hall, variety, vaudeville – whatever you will – has always been close to my form of theatre, the 'legitimate' theatre, as it is called. What a ridiculously stupid expression. 'Legitimate', 'straight' – does this mean that variety is 'illegitimate' and 'bent'? Why do we need to put everything into pigeonholes? Surely we are all one, we are all entertainers, from Henry Irving to George Robey.

Robey's diction was superb. Those music-hall boys had no mike and their consonants used to hit the back wall of the biggest theatre in the world *smack*. You never heard anybody say 'I couldn't hear' in those days.

The difference between the stand-up comic and the actor is that the comic has his colloquy with the audience. It is still two-way traffic, it's still a dialogue, not a monologue. The comic without his reaction is dead, so the audience must become his feed. To watch a truly great comedian perform is just as exciting, if not more so, than watching a fine Hamlet. The comic lives dangerously, he is always on the razor's edge. One moment of mistiming and his audience will turn on him. They are sitting there, waiting. Laughing – and waiting.

The music hall was nearer in atmosphere to the theatre of the last century than to that of today. Oranges were still consumed, peel everywhere, and the air sweet and sticky. Nuts were crunched under foot and the audience was constantly on the move from the bar to the lavatory and their seats. Some people just came in to see a favourite act and then depart again. It was rather like a cinema, I suppose, or television, but here the moving pictures could talk back, and here you could throw things at the moving pictures without being arrested. It was all part and parcel of the entertainment.

It is sad to think that by the time Archie Rice came along the music halls were nearly gone. There were just a handful left in England. The Chelsea Palace had become a store, the Collins Music Hall in Islington had become a wood yard, and the Met, Edgware Road, perhaps the most famous of them all, had disappeared into new architecture. Gone, all gone. Bingo halls and bowling alleys. The comedians had to find their way into the clubs or television. So there was not much left for me to observe. The music hall was crumbling, like the Empire, which, of course, was John's central point.

Getting inside Archie was not as easy as I had at first thought. There he was on paper saying, 'Come on, come and get me, I'm easy', waving a hat and raising his eyebrows. And indeed, to play him from the surface would have been simple – but a great disservice to John. I had to get under the bowler hat and behind the dead eyes.

Starting a part is always exciting, a journey into the unknown. There is always that slight tremor somewhere inside, not knowing what the end result is going to be. No matter how hard you work at preparing a part, nothing will really happen until you get into that empty rehearsal room and begin, nervously, to flex your muscles. This is where you start to blow into the character's mouth and see if the heart will begin to pump. No matter how experienced you are, the first get-together always makes the nerves jangle. There is always the inevitable chat beforehand, trying to postpone the moment when the scripts are opened and the author hears the lines for the first time other than in his head. Nobody knows if it is going to work, no matter how good you feel the piece is. The words have to stand up and be counted.

Everyone still putting off the moment. Banal banter, nobody really listening.

'Hullo, how lovely to see you.'

'And you . . . and you . . .'

'Have you seen Fred recently?'

'No, have you?'

'No . . .'

Pause.

'Pity.'

'Still drinking, I suppose.'

'I suppose . . .'

'Shame.'

'Could have done so many things.'

'She's left him.'

'Has she?'

'Long time now . . . can't say I blame her.'

What the hell are we talking about? *Who* the hell are we talking about? The stage manager indicates the coffee. Coffee is taken. Black, white, sugared, whatever.

'Biscuit?'

'Thanks.'

Crumbs in the mouth, coffee too hot. Perhaps it would be better if we didn't do a read-through. Nonsense. Why should I be nervous? I've done it all before a million times. I'm up there where a lot of people would like to be. I have no reason to be nervous, I'm a star. It's not working. I *am* nervous. I'm bloody nervous. Think of all the first nights, all the parts that I've played over the years. Think of . . . I mean I'm fifty, I've been at it for most of my life. I was born an actor. Look at it this way: *they* are nervous, *they* are the puppies, you're an old dog. Be quiet and drink the coffee.

'How's *The Sleeping Prince* . . . sorry, *Prince and the Showgirl* going?'

'Fine.'

'Finished?'

'Yes.'

'What was she like?'

'Mmmm?'

'Marilyn Monroe?'

'Oh.'

She must be nervous; otherwise she wouldn't be asking me these silly questions. Archie Rice, think about Archie Rice.

'I think she's very talented.'

'Yes.' Think whatever you like.

'Vulnerable?'

If only you knew. Is Archie Rice vulnerable? Has he got any talent? Did he have any talent? How aware is he of his position? Did he ever top the bill? Did he ever love Phoebe? Did he ever love himself? Suez . . . what did I think of Suez? Is that relevant? Everything is relevant.

'She's obviously much brighter than her publicity would have us believe.'

I must get a book on music-hall songs. I must go and see some more acts, bad ones. The pier, perhaps. I could try the pier. I'd really like to know what it feels like to be up there alone. It's not the same in Shakespeare. In Shakespeare when the soliloquy comes you're cosy in the character. The comic's up there all alone with his trousers down and wrapped up in his own personality.

'Was Miller around?'

Archie is vulnerable, very vulnerable. There's a big hook waiting in the wings.

'Marilyn Miller . . . not quite the same really, is it?'

Up there all alone looking at a sea of empty faces. Praying for the first laugh. Nothing coming back at you but cold breath. What's known as the comic's graveyard? Is it the Glasgow Empire? Must find out. Think it's somewhere up there.

'Funny combination, isn't it, Miller and Monroe?'

The temptation to be good is always going to be there; must remember to avoid it. Archie, when I get to him, has had it.

'Mind you, I thought Vivien was wonderful on stage.'

That really is the big problem: to be tatty, but entertaining at the same time.

'Vivien was divine.'

What would Archie have made of Marilyn Monroe? That would have been a meeting, those two together.

'Wonderful timing, and she looked so good.'

Wait a minute, perhaps they did meet. They could have been in the same show. Not Monroe – the character. The showgirl. Archie might well have fondled her breasts with his imagination. That's it, think along those lines.

What newspapers does he read? Does he read a newspaper? Of course he does. But does he read one daily? Yes. Why? To see if his name's in the obituary column.

'Have you ever thought of doing an Arthur Miller play?'

He's read a paper to keep up with events, political patter – always good for the act. Let them think you're brighter than they are. How does he vote? Has he ever voted? Perhaps not. That would be being too much part of the Establishment. That way the tax man would find him. The tax man *will* get him. His bogeyman.

'You'd be wonderful as Willy Loman.'

What does Archie drink? Draught Bass of course . . . of course. They don't have it in Canada, do they? He'll never survive in Canada, he'll never survive out of his own small pond. Archie Rice, he's . . .

'More coffee?'

It's happening, my God, it's happening. I'm beginning to fall in love with him. Tony Guthrie, it's happening all over again.

'Well, shall we sit down and read?'

We sat down, and Archie was alive. Archie Rice was on board and the train was pulling out of the station, destination unknown.

Of course, I had worked very hard at the text before the first reading, as I always do; but no matter how hard you work at it or how well you know the lines, you still have to take that first leap, and that doesn't happen until you meet your fellow actors. Then, and only then, can you get the true feel of your character, for it is then that he is seen through other people's eyes.

I often feel that you have to pick at the warts to find the real person, and in this Archie Rice was no exception. It is not a question of adding them; it is a question of dissecting them and seeing what is underneath. You can add them again afterwards if you want to. With Archie I really had to dig, and down in there I found gold. The gold that had been planted by John Osborne. It was like lighting a firework with a long fuse: a slow burner, but when it touched the gunpowder, the sky became a blaze of colour.

I learned to dance, I learned to sing like I thought Archie would, and I learned the loneliness of the stand-up comic.

The uninitiated might think that one of the most difficult things for me to attain was Archie's mediocrity. Sorry to disappoint you, but I can find plenty of that in myself. Everything inside the actor is geared to making things work successfully; the timing spot on, the singing correct and the dance routines perfect. Here everything had to be slightly out of kilter, and yet the actor inside me still had to hold on to the audience. It was a very exciting period, and a difficult one. Very exciting.

John took me around the music halls that were left, and I slowly began to piece together the background. The jigsaw began to fall into place.

To be able to do things badly, you first have to be able to do them very well, so my dancing went along the lines of Fred Astaire and my singing towards Mario Lanza. I slightly exaggerate, of course. I think, by the time I was ready, I could have made a decent attempt at standing up on my own and hurling someone else's patter at an unsuspecting audience in Hull. Or could I?

Step ball change, step ball change . . . it looks easy when you see them up there doing it, relaxed smile on the face, but believe me, it's not. Find the face in the audience, the woman who's going to giggle . . . where is she? Ah, there she is. Come on, laugh, you bugger, laugh. Here's a latecomer. Play off him, give yourself a minute to breathe. Pause, beat, pause, tag line. Not a titter – try again. 'Have you heard the one about . . . ?'

'Yes.'

Who said that? Ignore it, it will go away. 'Well, I'll tell you anyway.'

'No, thank you.'

Why doesn't he shut up? He's getting more laughs than me. Christ, I need a gin. A large one, several large ones. Should have had one before I came on here. I did. Perhaps that's the problem? Timing – nothing wrong with my timing. I'd be all right if that idiot would shut up. Give him his money back – send him home.

I'm dying up here. You're killing me, you bastard. You're throttling me. Get your hands off my throat, will you?

'Get off, you're rubbish.'

Think of something witty to say. Come on, you can do it. Say something.

'You're about as funny as my dog's arse.'

Someone shut him up. If I had a gun, I'd shoot him. If I had a machine gun, I'd shoot the lot.

'Bring the hook on and get him off.'

Why does everybody think he's so funny? Somebody's paying

him, that's what it is. He's in one of my rival's pockets. Cut-throat world, this. Somebody's after my job.

'He's drunk, I can smell the gin from here.'

If he doesn't shut up, I'll be off the circuit, and there aren't any others after this. I've gone right through the lot from the Palladium to the Scunthorpe Music Hall.

'Bring on the girls, give us some tits.'

That's not funny, that's not funny at all. What are they laughing at? Morons, all morons.

'Rubbish . . . rubbish . . .' He's chanting now.

That's all I need. In a minute they'll all join in. He's destroying my life. After this demonstration I'll be out of work, out of money and out of food. Doesn't he realize what he's doing?

'Come on, get on with it or get off . . .'

God, someone else has joined in. I'm going to be lynched.

'Come on.'

You think you're so clever you come up here and do it. Trouble is, he probably could. No, he couldn't. It's easy from down there, even *I* could do it from down there. Think of something, come on, think of something . . . nod at the conductor and get into the song and dance. That's it . . . right . . . music . . . come on, Bill, music.

Well, perhaps I'll leave it to those who have been schooled in it, those unsung Archie Rices who tread the boards of the clubs and halls, the holiday camps and the summer seasons. Those valiant troupers, that breed of vaudevillian who never become more than a pimple in the Hall of Fame. I take my hat off to the hero of the gin palace, the little man who is courageous enough to attempt to get a laugh out of a chunk of stone, the smiling jester who is for ever being pulled off by the managerial hook. I leave it to them.

Archie Rice was a landmark in my career and one that I'm very proud of. But, whatever is said about my performance, we must always look to the man who made it possible, the man who, with *Look Back in Anger*, *Luther* and *Inadmissible Evidence*, painted great, huge, exciting brushstrokes across the theatrical sky.

I sometimes thought of John Osborne as a young lion. Another such was Trevor Griffiths. John Dexter (one of my associate directors at the National Theatre, when it was still performing at the Old Vic in Waterloo Road, because the South Bank site had not yet been built) dropped a script on my desk one morning and said, 'Read that. You won't like it, but read it all the same. *I* think we should do it. *You* won't.' Clever John, he knew what he was at. First create a challenge, provoke, poke, stir, then sit back and see what happens. Naturally I read *The Party* immediately and found it fascinating. It was a political piece, but it wasn't overloaded by the author's political bias. He was too talented for that. There was no doubt that Trevor Griffiths had a considerable talent, and, to my mind, one that should be given the facilities of the National Theatre to stretch its muscles.

I suggested I should play the role of Tagg, not the leading part, but a very good one, and one with two enormous challenges for me: a twenty-minute speech and a Glaswegian accent.

This was to be my last performance in the Old Vic theatre, about which Joan said, 'If you do *King Lear* for it, I'll kill you' – and there was no point in going out the easy way. I have never been one for creeping out of the back door.

What I was not aware of at the time, or perhaps had not given it any thought, was that it was to be my last performance on any stage, professionally, that is. Strange, looking back now: would I have still made the same choice? Yes, I surely would. Point to the future always. Be positive and look ahead. Anyway, as far as I was concerned at the time, it was just my last appearance at the Old Vic. I still had many more boards to tread. I was already thinking about a Lear, and more.

I worked at the speech day and night for four months during the summer. I knew from experience that it was essential to get the words first. Then, when I'd got the words absolutely so that they were tripping off my tongue, I'd get the accent. Trying to learn the words and the accent at the same time was dreadfully unwise, for then you had twin problems to contend with. Every morning between six and eight I'd worry away at it like a terrier, slowly putting more lines into my head, inch by inch, word by word, syllable by syllable. Driving it into those old, decaying brain cells. I was sixty-four then, and the memory was not backing me up as it had in the old days. I began to bully myself like an irate schoolmaster: 'Come on, Olivier, it's not all that difficult. I mean you learnt James Tyrone two years ago, a much bigger part than this.'

'That was two years ago.'

On and on I went, any stray passer-by getting the script thrust into their unwilling hands. 'Just hear a bit of that, will you?' I was sure the weekend guests used to hide behind the bushes: 'Watch out, Larry's in the garden.' Slowly and painfully I got myself into order. The first rehearsal approached. I was determined to have it ready by then.

We all met in the rehearsal room at Aquinas Street, where the National Theatre offices were – Nissen huts – in those days. As I described earlier with *The Entertainer*, the usual first rehearsal jitters were in the air. Some actors can get so introverted they decide not to let you hear a word at all, every line directed at their jumper. I hasten to add I am not one of these; I just let it all out, regardless.

We started the reading and in time got round to my speech. I could sense that the company was waiting. Right, I thought, here goes. Down went the book and on came the speech. Here it was, here was the first hurdle. I plunged. I knew all eyes were on me. Twenty minutes later I had done it. Word bloody perfect. I can't quite remember, but I think there was a signal of appreciation.

The rehearsals appeared to go well, but the nearer we got to the first night, the further the lines seemed to go away. I knew them, by God I knew them, but did they know me?

In no time at all we were there, the first preview of my last performances at the Old Vic. The stage on which I'd played princes and kings over the years since 1937 was to greet me in 1973 as a Glaswegian revolutionary in a baggy suit. Really very comical, I suppose.

By the time I made my first entrance, the rest of the cast had been on for some time, and had settled. That cosy area under the warm spotlights had become their home for the evening. They were comfortable and at ease – or if they weren't, they appeared to be. Here was I, the newcomer, the intruder, the outsider in my crumpled suit, without any disguise but a Glaswegian accent. 'Here he is,' I could feel them thinking in the audience. 'All right, show us!' They probably weren't thinking that at all, but that's what I thought they were thinking. Laurence Olivier had entered their room thinly disguised as John Tagg. Word had got around that I was going to attempt to speak for twenty minutes, and they had come to see me roasting on the spit of my memory.

I sat down on the sofa, centre stage. I glanced out front . . . My God! were they checking their watches? There is always a fear when you've been at it for some time and have a certain amount of success that there is going to be someone in the audience who is seeing you for the first time and, after a bit, is going to turn to his companion and say, 'My dear, what is all the fuss about? *That* is Laurence Olivier?' This fear was with me now. There were bound to be people sitting out there who had never seen me before and, judging by the number of Japanese, had never even heard of me. Hands on my lap, looking perfectly relaxed (ha! always make them think that you are confident) . . . I started.

Twenty minutes is a long time, a very long time. I could feel the eyes of my company willing me on. The two brains started to work, the one saying the lines, the other in charge of the lines. This is John Tagg speaking, not Larry Olivier. Trevor Griffiths for John Tagg, John Dexter for John Tagg. Thirty seconds into the speech John Tagg takes over. Suddenly we are all together. That's what it's all about, give it to the man himself, let him talk, let *The Party* talk.

When the actor begins, it is the moment when the director and the author feel at their most vulnerable, for there is no longer anything they can do about it. Once the actor is up there on his side of the footlights, he and he alone is in charge. Good, bad or indifferent, he is the boss. The director and the author must remain silent: as far as they are concerned they are impotent, they may as well go home. You, the actor, are the 'guv'nor', and they must trust you. Weeks and weeks of rehearsing, rewriting, working are now being tried out up there where the actor belongs. He is in his territory, and nobody may enter save another actor.

The door at the back of the theatre opens, then shuts again. Someone has left. Who? John, Trevor? Doesn't matter now. I'm on the runway . . . I'm motoring.

'Don't get too confident, Olivier. That's when he'll get you, the bogeyman who steals the lines before they reach your lips. Have respect.'

'Must be halfway through. Not too many coughs. They're listening, by God, they're listening.'

Suddenly it was all over. I was at the other end of the tunnel and had crossed the tape that stretched over the author's vocabulary track. I'd gone through. I'd made the journey. I may not have been line perfect, but I'd got there. No night was easy with John Tagg, every performance was an immense challenge; but then, that is how it should be.

I trust that Trevor won't think I was more concerned about my speech than his play. His play is superb, and I'm sure will be done again and again. And I'm grateful that he gave me such an animal to fight with, night after night, as I prepared to say farewell to the Old Vic and the National.

I have talked in this chapter about two plays in particular, because they were both of special personal interest to me. *The Entertainer* marked my entry into new-wave theatre and also introduced me to the black-eyed actress who was to become my third wife. My choice of *The Party* for my exit naturally received much encouragement from Joan and John Dexter, both of whom had been protégés of Devine's Royal Court. In between, of course, there had occurred a major change in my life and career beginning with the directorship of the Chichester Festival Theatre in 1962 – and followed by the formation of the National Theatre Company in 1963. It was an exhilarating time; I had a new purpose, a new toy in the shape of the open stage, and the exciting task of planning the future.

George Devine had opened the way for me and I knew he would not mind if I purloined some of his best talents for my new enterprises. Apart from being a showcase for contemporary writers (Pinter, Wesker, Ionesco, Beckett, Osborne, etc.) the

Royal Court had produced a new breed of actors and directors
which it was my business to get to know. They included Albert
Finney, Alan Bates, Robert Stephens, Frank Finlay, Peter
O'Toole, William Gaskill and Joan Plowright; and, together with
Maggie Smith, Anthony Hopkins and Derek Jacobi, they came
to join my company at the National. Most of them were part of
the influx of regional talent in the 1960s (when the Beatles took
the world by storm). They had a reality, inventiveness and
spontaneity which brought richness and variey to the stage; I
sensed immediately that they made the sort of company I had
around me at the St James's look a wee bit old-fashioned. Once
a thing has been done in a fresh style and manner the atmosphere
becomes charged with it and you can't escape breathing it into
your lungs. Of course acting styles change about every fifteen
years, and in Britain they are invariably linked with social and
political change. Any young English actor with a public school
background and a much-too-upper-class accent was going to
have a hard time of it for the next fifteen years or so. (Not a
few of them would resort to disowning their families and claiming
a Cockney barmaid for a mother!)

As Tynan wrote of Osborne's generation:

For the first time I was recognising people on stage that I'd
lived with, that I'd shared bedsitting rooms with, that I'd
queued for buses with, that I'd been in the local amateur
dramatic society with in my home town, Birmingham. For the
first time my own generation was on stage, not by tolerance
but by right, saying the kind of things we'd spent nights at
the university arguing about; but now saying them in public
to an audience that wasn't used to hearing them . . . They
were a fully educated generation. They'd been in their early
teens, I suppose, during the first post-war Labour govern-
ments and they'd come to maturity with no doubt in their
minds that they had a stake in the country's future. They had
a stake in what society meant and was going to do, and they
were no longer prepared to be admitted to the arts on
sufferance; the arts were their business and their business
was the arts.

This new breed of actors was, in part, a product of their new material, but I felt myself most happily in tune with many of their qualities. It remained to be seen whether they could perform with equal success in the classics. But my instincts told me that a judicious combination of the old with the new was the only way to achieve the kind of acting ensemble I was determined to form. All my life I had struggled to raise the audiences' consciousness and appreciation of acting as an art, not merely an interpretive craft. It was to be one of my main goals at the National Theatre.

THIRTEEN

COLOSSUS OF THE DRAMA

Eugene O'Neill is the father figure of modern American drama: his shadow touches all the modern American playwrights from Tennessee Williams and Arthur Miller to Sam Shepherd and David Mamet, as well as a great many British playwrights. O'Neill was a colossus of twentieth-century drama: he dared and succeeded.

His wife describes how he wouldn't talk to her for weeks and weeks when he was writing, but would lock himself away. If he did come down to lunch or to a meal, he'd just sit there, forking up odd bits, his eyes red with weeping. Though all playwrights must write from a certain amount of actual experience, I always felt that O'Neill had really done everything he described.

He put his true experiences on paper and so it looked like an early photograph, all sepia and misty, past memories, the biographical playwright.

He was a writer with a heart the size of a melon, which he sliced open from time to time and dipped his pen in. I suppose it is not surprising that he would not let *Long Day's Journey into Night* be performed until after his death. It was too close and too personal, too much blood and pain, though it must have been odd never to see your masterpiece performed. A musician with all the sounds in his head and no instrument to play them on, a bit like Beethoven, I suppose. All the same, something inside him must have regretted that. But then again, to spill your life out on to a stage and say 'This is how it was' can't be easy. And when the raw truth is spoken, as I believe it is in this play, nobody really wants criticism.

He must have thought a lot about the reaction it would cause, for he knew that people would want to see it as soon as they possibly could. Indeed he must have wanted the world to look at him, otherwise he couldn't have written it, or he would have burnt it as each page left the typewriter.

It was almost as though he was saying, 'There, that's what it was like, that's what it was really like, that's the pain that I've lived with all my life. You may call me a romantic but I know that I'm a realist. You think I choke on my imagination, I have no imagination, my brain is burning with only true, stark facts.'

It is fascinating to look at his early work and see the playwright emerging. It was very raw and the brushwork naïve. He splashed ideas and imagination on paper with, it would seem, no respect for proscenium or theatrical format at all. He wrote movies for the stage. 'Scene One: a boat in the Caribbean' – that sort of thing. No more your French windows and your polite cups of tea. A boat in the Caribbean, a dockside bar in London. Fog and whores, pimps and pressgangs. He put the sea on the stage, the moon and the stars, engine-room oil and death. Warts, spots and boils, they were all there. He exploded a theatrical myth and went back to the basics. He put the earth back into the theatre and made you smell the sweat.

From *Long Voyage Home* through to *Long Day's Journey* the development of the writer is incredible; and yet you can see the same hand in both, pen poised ready to jab like a sword.

In his middle plays you can see the young man and the mature man walking side by side, hand in hand; eventually, in the later plays, the mature man tells the young man to hold his peace and not pop up every now and again like a jack-in-the-box. The older man's pen slowly pushes aside the pencil of the boy O'Neill who passaged the world in a boat, gazed at the stars and dreamed of what would be.

He was every inch a writer, and I think we are very fortunate that he did not put his work down in the form of novels, which at the time would have seemed the obvious way to go. I mean, if you want sea, stars, moons and fog, you go straight to the novel form – but not O'Neill. He was, of course, familiar with the theatrical format, his father being an actor.

I was about to say it couldn't have been easy having an actor for a father and then realized that, having four children of my own, I was pointing a finger at my mirror. I think what I meant was, it couldn't have been easy having *that* actor for a father. No . . . maybe I shouldn't have said that either. Never mind, I've said it now.

Of course one is only allowed to look at O'Neill's father through O'Neill's eyes. Perhaps the old man wasn't so bad after all. He was rather successful, and they did live in a certain amount of comfort. Maybe O'Neill felt bitter because his father hadn't fulfilled his potential and had opted out for what might have seemed easy money. But then again, maybe the father did fulfil his potential, and that was as far as he was going to go anyway.

Whatever, the man who created modern American drama was given to us by that father and mother; the actor and the drug addict. It is interesting to think that the background that bred him was that of a maker of illusions and a taker of illusions. Does that say something about all of us, I wonder?

It was suggested, again by Kenneth Tynan, that I play James Tyrone in *Long Day's Journey into Night* in the early days of the National. But I didn't want to do it. I was wary of the role, having seen Fredric March play it in the original production. It wasn't that March put me off, though it was a giant performance to follow; it was that I didn't really want to play the part of an actor. I sensed that I would be very good in the role, but something kept telling me not to. I felt a strong resistance to playing an actor and yet, strangely enough, I'd happily produced a play about one some time before at the St James's, *Winter Journey*, in which Michael Redgrave gave a superb performance as the alcoholic. Quite frightening and true.

Why is it that, when he is given life under the author's pen, the poor old Thespian is invariably portrayed as a drunk? We're not all like that, you know. I have known some sober ones in my time. In fact I've actually met some teetotal ones . . . not many, but some.

However, in 1971, I decided to take on this marathon, partly aided by Tynan, but also forced by a decline in funds at the Old Vic. It seemed the ideal play to put on at the time, if we were to be frugal. One set and five in the cast. So the great god Money, and Ken, won.

Looking at it romantically – and why not? – O'Neill stretched his hand across the Atlantic and put us back in motion again.

So, not for the first time, lack of funds set me off in a new direction. The rogue and vagabond with his box of tricks and his sticks of paint always worked harder when the upturned hat was empty.

I'll never regret James Tyrone, and would have been very sad to have missed him. But then, if I'd not played him, I would have never known. Strange how parts can turn on you, consume you, regurgitate you, and make you ask yourself why you had any doubts in the first place.

It was a long part. The cast met once a week for five weeks to talk about *Long Day's Journey* and to read it through; this encouraged us to think about our parts all the time, mulling them over, dreaming about them. It is not the amount of times you've rehearsed, but the length of time it's been in your heart that is crucial.

If you play an actor, you have to be a bit florid, a bit theatrical, and even with all that the audience may not be quite sure if it's you, or the part you are playing. I gave the part twelve lines of Shakespeare, quite short, but enough to assert my role as an actor, enough to create that stillness you need in the theatre.

Long Day's Journey into Night is without question O'Neill's masterpiece. Infinitely better than *The Iceman Cometh*, where he went overboard and tried to outdo himself. The part of Tyrone is one of the richest ever written: very long but nearly perfect. The repetition's a challenge, a delicious little problem to overcome, but then I enjoy challenges.

As it turned out, it became a huge success and seemed to be the beginning of a new era for the National Theatre's coffers: we became the darlings of the subsidized theatre. The swings and roundabouts of West End fashion had stopped at our particular door. We followed it quickly with Tom Stoppard's *Jumpers,*

The Front Page and *The Misanthrope*. We were back on top
again.

It's strange how the public and the critics (maybe the public
because of the critics) sway from one major company to the
other. Today the National Theatre is flavour of the month,
tomorrow the Royal Shakespeare. Nothing wrong with it, of
course. Rivalry in the theatre is very healthy and can only lead
to superior work. But what the fans sometimes forget is that it
is the same pool of actors moving back and forth across the
river, depending which company is offering the better parts.
There are loyalties, of course, and these seem to remain with
the actor's original theatre – in my case the Old Vic, which
eventually became the National.

The rivalries have always been there, and have been encouraged by the public and critics alike. You can list them from
Shakespeare's day, and historians could obviously go back
further. The Globe and the Bear then, later, the Theatre Royal
and Covent Garden, then on to the Lyceum and Her Majesty's,
followed by the Old Vic and the Stratford Memorial, to the
present day.

It is interesting to note that there have always been two major
companies around, where at some time or other you will be able
to watch the leading actors of the day. Even those who have
been lured away by the beckoning monetary hand of the silver
screen will always come back again, just to dip their roots in the
hormone powder of their beginnings. Well, almost all, anyway,
those who really believe that they owe the empty boards a
thanks or two. Those who have not returned probably didn't
have it in the first place, and are welcome to their bear pits in
Beverly Hills.

PART FOUR

THE SILVER SCREEN

FOURTEEN

EARLY HOLLYWOOD

When I went to Hollywood in 1930, aged twenty-three, I was very snooty about moving pictures. I went for the money – it was the Depression – and the chance of fame: to have a go at something different, rewarding or not. More likely not.

The Jazz Singer, the first 'talkie', had been released in 1927, and the studios were desperate for actors who had good voices. I considered myself a Shakespearean actor and I was sure I could out-talk anyone. I still didn't have great confidence in my looks, but RKO had seen me as Beau Geste in a London stage production, directed by the fearsome Basil Dean, and they thought I was rather dashing and would be another Ronald Colman on their books. In fact, I'd slavishly modelled my stage appearance on Colman's in his silent film. Basil Dean, a master of spectacular productions, based his whole concept of the play on the film; one medium aping another, with the usual disastrous results. He had a bad reputation for his bastard bullying methods. He bullied me to his heart's content. I was lost among the hundred legionnaires, the smoke, the real sparks of fire, all that timber of the massive sets; and he screamed at me from the dress circle of Her Majesty's, 'Show us some charm, boy. More charm, boy!' My performance badly needed some big close-ups.

I knew even then, I think, that no one, not even Douglas Fairbanks, could match Ronald Colman's screen close-ups. They were marvellous because he had a beautiful face, and because he had a deep but gentle masculinity: the ideal of the dark

Englishman. In all my acting up to then, especially at the Birmingham Rep, I'd taken pride in submerging my personality so that the audience wouldn't recognize 'me' in one part after another. I went to Hollywood with no great confidence in my personality. I might become a star, I was sure I could act and I had what was thought to be essential in the earliest talkies, an English accent.

RKO gave me no great acting parts, and I gave them no marvellous close-ups. I could talk all right, but my performances were precious, lacking in vitality, charmless. But I felt comparatively at ease in my last film for RKO – *Westward Passage* with Ann Harding – and Greta Garbo liked my performance. She asked me to be her leading man in *Queen Christina* and, naturally, I accepted. What a breakthrough! But, after two weeks on the set, she'd found me out. The director wanted to shoot a love scene first, which was Hollywood logic, I suppose, to see if the lovers jelled before too much money was spent; but it unsettled me. I took Garbo in my arms to 'awaken her passion'. There was no famous flicker of an eyelid or of the corner of her mouth, however faint; only shyness and cold eyes. I was miserable and overacted. She became bored with my twitchiness and saw my lack of personality, a mouse to her lioness. All the great screen double acts had equal personality: Tracy and Hepburn, Bogart and Bacall, Garbo and John Gilbert.

'We want you to know, Larry,' said Walter Wanger, the producer, when he fired me from the picture, 'we're all crazy about you here at Metro.' He tried to make me feel better by offering me a screen test for Romeo to Norma Shearer's Juliet. 'I don't believe in Shakespeare on the screen,' I said, and left Hollywood. Ronald Colman stayed, thrilled audiences with his voice, doubled his charm when he talked, and won an Oscar for his brilliant performance in George Cukor's *A Double Life* – the story of an actor playing Othello on the stage who takes his work home with him with disastrous results. (Alas, this was one of Vivien's abiding problems.) I went back to the stage and to films in England, trying hard for variety, and leaving my work in the dressing room or the studio. I saw *Queen Christina* and thanked my lucky stars I'd been turned down by the greatest star of them all. The part was a bad one, and I wouldn't have had a hope in it. It was simply a bad part; even Gilbert didn't manage to make anything of it. Fancy having a bad performance immortalized in a Garbo film!

Ronald Colman became a dear friend, and he revealed his sweet and honest nature. Vivien and I honeymooned on his yacht *The Dragoon*. Years later, George Cukor – another friend and hard-working professional – told me Garbo was upset at the way I'd been treated. I asked him to get a message to her in retirement: 'I applaud you for getting rid of me. I have no bitterness. Only admiration.'

English films in the 1930s were cast with London stage actors, and Alexander Korda, who wanted an English Hollywood, had more grand ideas than most on either side of the Atlantic. But he gave me opportunities, which I only took disdainfully because I still despised the medium; I felt unhappy in it, and was using most of my energy trying to build strong performances on the stage in the evenings, after shooting all day in the studios. Korda's English crews and electricians, too, thought films were inconsiderable because they were to do with an ephemeral and untrustworthy thing called entertainment. They had not learnt respect for the medium. Hollywood, along with every other place in America, had a healthy respect for money; and if movies made money, boy, they deserved respect. A much healthier attitude. If you want to be a happy film actor or technician, get rid of your snobbery.

While I was giving a 'real' and bravura performance of Mercutio on the stage to John Gielgud's Romeo (we were alternating the roles), I was trying to play Orlando in a film version of *As You Like It* to a Rosalind with a German accent, whose impersonation of a boy hardly attempted to deceive the audience; but they loved her whatever she did. I made my humble most of Orlando but the circumstances were too much charged against me. The director's flocks of sheep ran away with the film, and if Walter Wanger had asked me what I was doing in such a mess I would've had to say, as Ralph Richardson did, 'Getting £600 a week.' (Tax five-sixths of that, of course.) Korda provided me with a very good costume part in *Fire Over England* with Vivien (and

Flora Robson as Queen Elizabeth), but I emoted too much and, in the American version, they had to cut one of my scenes because the New York preview audience got the giggles.

Then along came a man who pulled me up by the jockstrap and dragged me down to earth! If any film actor is having trouble with his career, can't master the medium and, anyway, wonders whether it's worth it, let him pray to meet a man like William Wyler. In 1938, when war was rumbling and I was still worrying about how bad my face looked on the screen, I received a telegram: ARE YOU INTERESTED GOLDWYN IDEA FOR VIVIEN YOURSELF AND OBERON IN WUTHERING HEIGHTS? This wasn't enough to get me back on the first boat and train to dreadful Hollywood, because it smelt of Goldwyn corn – with a pinch of Merle Oberon tartness – and Vivien was to play Isabella, not Cathy, which certainly didn't fit into the way she should have been planning her career. Slowly we were learning that actors have to manipulate their careers with cool, determined heads.

Then the excellent script arrived: very versatile, very American, by Ben Hecht and Charles MacArthur, who wrote *The Front Page*. But I still wasn't won over, for what is any Hollywood film against a grand Victorian novel?

William Wyler then came in person to see me, perfectly charming and obviously in love with his medium. Although at first he struck me as being a little naïve, he did seem to understand the character of Heathcliff. I too had done my homework this time. I'd learnt that from Garbo, who had known everything there was to know about Queen Christina. But I still said no. I went to see his current success, *Jezebel*, and realized that he had a telling way with camera and with dialogue. Vivien saw that I liked Wyler, liked the part of Heathcliff, and persuaded me. Often your partner's head is cooler than yours. But she'd never had a wretched time in Hollywood.

What happened on the *Wuthering Heights* set is well known. I'm glad. Whereas Garbo was cold, Wyler was vicious: a Hollywood version of the nasty Basil Dean. At about this time I'd had a God-given blinding flash – not from anything Willie Wyler said – about my God-damned face. Just take it, settle for it and use it; and stop thinking about it, because it's spoiling your acting.

There wasn't a great deal of paint around in Hollywood in those days, and for *Wuthering Heights* they just daubed my face here and there; I decided to forget about my image, to give the role a true personality. Flora Robson, who played Ellen, and I more or less mastered the Yorkshire accent – who were the Americans to argue about that? – so I felt unfettered and gave my all to the emotional, passionate, disdainful and arrogant Heathcliff. The vicious Wyler just kept on saying 'Lousy' and told me to do it again and again, without explanation, while giving Merle Oberon all the attention she wanted.

Wily old Wyler was softening me up. With the occasional violent ego-blow: 'That was lousy overacting. What dimension have you climbed up to now? Get off your arse and come down from that cloud. Crawl back down here to earth and join us.' It was probably then that I said his medium was too anaemic to take great acting, which shows how pompous and opinionated I was, although I remember with absolute horror hearing myself say those words. Wyler was a marvellous sneerer, debunker; and he brought me down. I knew nothing of film acting or that I had to learn its technique; it took a long time and several unhandsome degrees of the torture of his sarcasm before I realized it. 'Do you think you could try seeing if our little medium could capture one of your frowns instead of a frown and a glare?' He knew I couldn't be told anything. He knew I'd come to my senses, in time, to some true feeling. Very flattering. I didn't know it at the time. I merely thought him a cruel bastard!

Wyler was a professional. He liked me, and enjoyed talking to me at his house in the evenings. (Or was he trying to prevent my catharsis happening on the set? His cunning was quite up to that.) 'I want you to be patient about this,' he'd say. 'But you're quite wrong to take up this despising attitude. I believe with my heart and soul this is the greatest medium ever invented in the field of expression. There's nothing in literature, Greek drama, in anything you like, be it the most primitive, which is beyond it. If you put your mind to it. Don't sneer at that *As You Like It* Shakespeare film. Shakespeare can be done as anybody else can be done if you just think out how. Just think and keep thinking. Do it right, and *anything* can be done on film. Don't worry about your personality, just get on with getting on with your medium, and acting. Regard the camera as another actor, if you like, who shows the audience your subtlest reactions. And don't bring your personal problems to the set.'

He was right – again. I think I was being high-handed because my emotions were in a bit of a whirl. I was most deeply in love with Vivien, and I could think of little else. Merle and I had been spitting at each other all day, in real hate, and he suddenly made us do a love scene, which went beautifully in one take. The camera does lie sometimes, but it doesn't like lies, insincerity or superficiality in others. It loves true feeling and isn't too concerned about what goes on on the surface, provided it's subtle. OK, tricks of the trade. OK, it's an art. What Willie Wyler was really trying to teach me was humility. I'll say it now – instead of at the end – as a homage to him: my stage successes have provided me with the greatest moments outside myself; my film successes the best moments, professionally, within myself.

Wuthering Heights was a success. I had my catharsis; Merle and Willie and I became friends and the only Goldwyn corn was the heather on the Yorkshire moors, which was as high as an elephant's eye. When I had asked Ralph whether I should take the part or not, when I had first been offered it, he had said, 'Yes, dear boy. Bit of fame. Good.' In Hollywood, fame meant power. Then came Darcy in *Pride and Prejudice* for MGM, which I accepted because Vivien was to be my co-star and George Cukor the director. But no. Greer Garson became Elizabeth Bennett and Robert Z. Leonard the director, and I was very unhappy with the picture. It was difficult to make Darcy into anything more than an unattractive-looking prig, and darling Greer seemed to me all wrong as Elizabeth. To me, Jane Austen had made Elizabeth different from her affected, idiotic sisters; she was the only down-to-earth one, but Greer played her as the most affected and silly of the lot. I also thought that the best points in the book were missed, although apparently no one else did. I'm still signing autographs over Darcy's large left lapel. MGM always got their costumes right.

The story goes that David Selznick was reading Daphne du

Maurier's *Rebecca* in bed (he'd read at least one other book, *Gone with the Wind*). When the description of Max de Winter's face came along – 'arresting, sensitive and mediaeval in some strange, inexplicable way . . .' (I hate playing inexplicable characters) – he wrote my name in the margin. If true, this shows my face had become my fortune and I was no longer the poor man's Ronald Colman. Selznick was also shrewd enough to choose an Englishman to direct, Alfred Hitchcock, who was wise enough to choose an English cast and to advise me to grey up my temples because, at thirty-two, I looked too young. I admired and liked Hitchcock tremendously, and we had a jolly time; all English pros together. He didn't treat us like cattle – although he boasted that that was what he thought about all actors, and although my leading lady to my mind implacably qualified as a female of that species. I loved his little bits of business and the way he always avoided the obvious. Do you remember the confrontation scene in the sitting room in that seaside hut? Instead of plonking me in the obvious big armchair, he put me around a corner in the shadows where the girl – Joan Fontaine – had to find me. But he didn't give me much help with the part.

I could manage the smooth, impervious Englishman; but the haunted quality, the mystery element, was thinly written. I was used to tragedy; this was melodrama. I couldn't find the reality of the part. Joan Fontaine played the girl beautifully but I was never sure how much she was to be deceived; nor indeed how much the audience were to be deceived. When Joan wore a copy of Rebecca's dress, for example, which was a childish mistake wickedly suggested to her by Mrs Danvers, was I meant to be cross or furiously angry? But why? What about?

I had not been happy with Wyler but he had taught me more than I knew. When Alexander Korda came to Hollywood with the script of *Lady Hamilton* and a juicy offer which would mean security for a few months, I decided to accept, although the war had now started. I succumbed to the Hungarian's patriotic zeal and played the English hero, Lord Nelson, not as the neurotic I discovered in my researches, but as the gallant yet gentle sailor in the patriotic convention of the times. Nelson had the most extraordinary girlish mouth, so I wore rose lips because I was now becoming relatively at ease in the medium, didn't have a star's face that couldn't be changed from one film to the next, and wanted to practise my craft of acting.

Korda, with his cultural knowledge, was a particularly sophisticated director; he had ideas and the acumen to put them into practice. A highly practical man.

I then returned to England to join the Fleet Air Arm. They'd bring us actors down from time to time to make Ministry of Information films and I was released for *49th Parallel*, a film with a patriotic theme directed by the imaginative Michael Powell who allowed actors to act. I was happy with my simple and gentle French-Canadian trapper, which I established in only ten minutes' screen time. Had I learnt something about the economy and directness of film acting from my days in Hollywood?

FIFTEEN

SHAKESPEARE ON FILM

I have been luckier than most because I was ultimately given the opportunity to take Shakespeare from the wooden O and place him on the silver screen. 'Not possible,' I was told. Initial attempts to do this had been absolutely appalling. The audiences had stayed away in their multitudes. But I had the good fortune to be something of a movie star; I already had a following, so whatever I did was looked upon with curiosity. Somehow it worked, and I think it had much to do with the way I adapted the sound of the lines to the modern ear. The film-going public, many of whom had never been in a theatre in their lives, understood, enjoyed and were entertained. I appealed to a new public, to those who had thought that Shakespeare was 'not for the likes of them'. When actor and audience communicate well, the sense of freedom is unbelievable. It is like flying together. Once the public had been wooed and won by *Henry V*, the critics and the studios came round to the idea that it was possible to put Shakespeare on the screen. *Henry* was a box-office success. Shakespeare had been given to the people. He was no longer for a small band of the select. Film, of course, can never give the actor the real sense of urgency that happens between curtain rising and curtain falling, but it can project a man's thoughts to millions of people who would never have had the opportunity to hear them had they simply remained upon a stage.

From the beginning of England's war with Germany, I realize

now, I was being tuned up for the undreamt-of film of *Henry V*.
As I flew over the country in my Walrus I kept seeing it as
Shakespeare's sceptred isle. I was thirty-seven and in fine fettle.
I asked Wyler to direct but he said, 'No, if it's Shakespeare it
must be you.' So I went away and thought and thought about
what was practicable. I could think of the play sideways, upwards
and outwards, because I knew it backwards. I saw its nuances
of rhythm and movement in my mind's eye, and then heard its
dialogue.

In *Henry V* more than any other, Shakespeare moans about
the confines of his Globe Theatre – 'or may we cram/Within
this wooden O the very casques/That did affright the air at
Agincourt?' – and all those short battle scenes, in a lot of his
plays, are frustrated cinema. I was amazed how easily I thought
in the language of film: panorama shots, tracking shots, dolly
shots, medium short, close-ups, and the movement and prying
of the camera. Flash upon flash came the problems. Flash upon
– no, perhaps a little longer – came the solutions. How I loved
the problems! How I loved the medium's ingenuity! How I loved
the medium! Wyler's medium, mine, William Shakespeare's.
The main problem, of course, was to find a style which Shakespearean actors could act and yet which would be acceptable to
the audience of the time, used to little other than the most
obvious propaganda.

I've sometimes been lucky in my thoughts. 'You've been lucky
in your friends, too, dear boy,' Ralph would say. During the
preparations for the shooting of *Henry V* I was acting in a
film called *Demi-Paradise*, directed by Anthony Asquith, who'd
directed Wendy Hiller's *Pygmalion* and many other things English. Under his sensitive direction I played another gentle and
bewildered person – this time a Russian visiting England – but
it was an undemanding part. Asquith was not a demanding man,
and he was happy to help me gather my *Henry V* crew of film
technicians, a happy band of brothers because they were fired
by my enthusiasm and I seemed to know what I was talking
about. Filippo del Giudice – bless him – was the moving force
behind the project; an Italian interned by the English for the first
four months of the war, he kept all financial worries from me

and left me with complete artistic control, including every bit of casting.

What sort of man was Shakespeare's Chorus to be, narrating and commenting his way through the play, showing his frustration that the Globe audience weren't in France? Get rid of him altogether? Have him as a voice-over, appearing at the end to wrap up the show? Ah! No voice-over, but if the Chorus at the end, why not at the beginning as well, where Shakespeare put him? And in the Globe, as Shakespeare had him. And then I wouldn't have to cut his question: 'can this cockpit hold/The vasty fields of France?' The goddamn play was telling me the style of the film.

Dress the Chorus as an Elizabethan actor (which he was), get him – with broad gestures – to challenge the imaginations of the unruly audience in the cockpit. Maybe that way the film audience would be challenged. Play the first few scenes on the Globe stage in a highly, absolutely deliberate, theatrical style; get the film audience used to the language, and let them laugh its excesses out of their systems before the story really begins. I was determined to bring in the comics, Falstaff and his friends Nym, Bardolf and Pistol, for without them, it would have been two and a half hours of Henry, Henry, Henry: the film cried out for light relief!

Henry, historically and in Shakespeare's eyes, had an unheroic beginning, so I would start with me, the Elizabethan actor playing Henry, waiting in the wings, while the audience got to know the other characters, especially Pistol and his wife, the former Mistress Quickly. Bring on Falstaff, give him some lines from *Henry IV Part II* and to hell with the purists, because he was a leader of the comics, an old friend of Henry's, and later, Mistress Quickly tells us of his death. I wanted the audience – the universal audience – to have a concrete image of the dear old man. Surprise, surprise, the purists approved.

'If you really want to shock or delight an audience, get them a little bored first,' said William Wyler. You need some confidence and courage to take such advice – maybe not, just be true to your instincts – but I wanted the film audience to get a restless feeling of being crabbed and confined in the Globe's

wooden O, irritated by the silly actors speaking in their exaggerated way, so that when we at last leave the place, with a flourish
of William Walton's music, and I speak my lines beginning with
'Now sits the wind fair, and we will aboard' realistically and
with a modern tone, there's a tremendous feeling of relief and
anticipation. The language may be archaic, but it's not strange.
It's charming. It's sincere.

But how to make the language seem real all the way through?
To the end of the story. One of the original ideas was to use
Kenilworth Castle for the French settings. Lovely. But all that
stone, dust and patchy grass would seem too familiar, too real
to a modern audience, who'd be thinking: 'OK. Henry's taken
us away from the bloody Globe and given us a new set of
costumes to look at, and that "fair wind" speech was good, but
aren't they still talking poetic gobbledegook?' I didn't want the
eye to quarrel with the ear; what the eye saw had to bolster the
seeming reality of the language. No eyesore like crumbling
Kenilworth stone; but something artificial, very pretty and
unreal, and yet real to the mind's eye's vision of a romantic tale
of an heroic mediaeval king. Oh, how I prayed to God – or to
the Willies, Shakespeare and Wyler – that I would have the
courage to be absolutely true to that vision: not fudge it. Then,
out of the sometimes divine collaboration between expert art
designers (Paul Sheriff, Carmen Dillon and Roger Furse – my
thanks to them) and a director with a vision, I decided to
base the costumes and scenery very meticulously on mediaeval
illustrations in story books, especially those of the Limburg
brothers, with their bright and pastel colours, prettiness, odd
perspectives and, sometimes, no perspectives at all. I wanted
the characters to spring out from the beautiful, stylized, almost
cut-out scenery, alive and kicking and speaking in a vigorous
and varied language; the actors to dominate, to feel confident
and sometimes to dwarf the scenery. Thus, when I'm telling the
audience the wind's set fair for France, I'm standing at the mast
of a miniature and colourful ship soon to approach the French
town of Harfleur, which is miniature, pretty and an odd shape –
undaunting to the characters, uninhibiting to the actors and
intriguing to the audience.

'Action!' The power and responsibility of a film director direct-ing two actors from his canvas-backed throne, or two thousand from behind a tracking camera, can be awesome: sometimes his ego drives him into arrogance or a dreadful feeling of vulner-ability. Not with *Henry V*, though. There we were, a band of artists and technicians, humble in our souls because Hitler was killing our countrymen, imbued with a sense of history, gallantly overcoming wartime shortages and problems. We had no quick-cranking Technicolor camera to slow down the smoke from the chimneys or the tidal waves in the Thames on the model of Elizabethan London at the beginning of the film. Horses were as rare as kingdoms, but how we loved our problems and revelled in our resourcefulness! We were inspired by the warmth, humanity, wisdom and Britishness just beneath the surface of Shakespeare's brilliant jingoism. (The play has its Welshman and Irishman, too, as well as the former Mistress Quickly.) And there I was, an Englishman with a mission to bring Shakespeare to the screen, to bring caviare to the general audience; not in a snobbish sense, but because I love caviare. Both it and Shakespeare's esoteric nature are overrated, and it's certainly not Shakespeare's fault it's not for more universal consumption. (He'd be writing a new 'Carry On' series for Channel 4, or soap-opera cameo parts for ageing actors now, if he were around.) I had a mission; I was physically and emotionally very fit; I'd learnt about co-ordination and balance while flying my Walrus; my country was at war; I felt Shakespeare within me, I felt the cinema within him. I knew what I wanted to do, what he would have done, and every sinew was stiffened because the budget was so tight. Between 'Action!' and 'Cut!' things went very smoothly, with only the usual number of cock-ups. No temper. The war cleared the head, but it was love of the medium – my band of brothers', mine, Shakespeare's, Wyler's, the modern audience's – which summoned most of the blood.

However, I did not direct like Wyler. I would not have had enough film in my stock room to have someone come down from the stairs, pause at the newel post and walk off just right of the camera sixty-three times, something which he made me do. I mapped out every movement first and knew exactly what every shot was going to be. I couldn't afford to re-shoot, so I designed every angle in advance, knew every move, every cut; all was pre-timed and pre-planned.

We'd found a setting for Shakespeare's dialogue. Now we had to find out how to create a Shakespearean battle sequence, free from the fetters of the wooden O and made up of short scenes, yet full of his drama, reality and humanity. I was particularly anxious to maintain purity of intention in the way the scenes were handled. I felt myself to be an agent of his imagination. I looked at the old masters like Eisenstein and D. W. Griffith for inspiration, but saw that only Shakespeare's spirit and the spirit of his drama and characters (from the comics to the heroic king himself) could conjure up the stirring images and the unique pattern, rhythm and movement of the screen's first Shakespearean battle: a battle which encompasses typical Shakespearean twists of high seriousness and low comedy. The telegraph poles, the pylons, the grey and stunted foliage, meant there were no mediaeval battlefields in England, and no horses. So, we went to Ireland, where I lived in a caravan like a modern field commander, ordered the day's shooting like military manoeuvres, co-ordinated and played my roles of director, producer, leading actor, editor and script editor with gusto and sincerity and, with 150 willing Irish horsemen and 500 willing Irish foot men, worked for six hard weeks to produce ten minutes of film action.

Every second, half second, of that action was clearly in my head before the six weeks' action began. I invented the charge of the French cavalry for reasons of pace, rhythm and conflict, and because Shakespeare probably would have done so – better: my small, but confident, talent's homage to his expansive genius. I shot the charge with an exciting tracking shot, full of technical problems almost on the pinnacle of the imaginative concept itself. I added Walton's music and realistic sound effects; and when the dramatic action needed a pause, I sent the sound of a thousand arrows through the air.

There was, at least, one insuperable problem. I made the soldiers on both sides fight vigorously and realistically – no backs to the audience stuff – but I showed no bloody gashes. The bright mediaeval costumes tended, too, to emphasize the formal elements and patterns of the battle. But to be true to the film's overall style the battle should have been fought on green velvet – and that, clearly, was impracticable. Once again the play itself saved us. Between the pretty parts in the French palaces and the Battle of Agincourt, Shakespeare has a long and contemplative night sequence, which gave the screen neutral colours and tones to cushion the contrast between the artificiality of mediaeval picture-book castles and the earthiness of Irish fields, pretty and green though they were.

I always looked to the text of the play to give me the movements of the camera, and towards the end of that night sequence I had the camera look through Henry's eyes as he reviews his thoughts and the serried ranks of his soldiers, then cut away to see him climb into a cart and then come into a big close-up as he says: '. . . Now, soldiers, march away/And how thou pleasest, God, dispose the day!' Not a few moments before, Henry has been talking about Saint Crispin's day, so the audience's mind is truly attuned to a day of death or glory; and its eye – as it turned out – would not be offended by the day's stylistic change of setting. I feel Shakespeare and God disposed the day well. They got us over a stylistic anachronism which grieved only the pedantic and mean-spirited. We had faith in what was practicable. If it comes off, it's good. If it's practicable, it can be exciting – given the spirit and the faith.

In the early days of preparation I puzzled about previous failures of Shakespeare on the screen, worried about his verse and worried about the Shakespearean actors who were to speak it. Even earlier, when I had been flying my Walrus, I said to myself, 'This flying is going to help my acting if I ever get back to it.' I was perfectly all right in my physical coordination – some actors aren't, you know – but as I sat in front of the controls, very basic controls which bound you very close to the aircraft's behaviour, my mental co-ordination was all askew, giving me and my Walrus rough rides and crude movements; relaxing too much on to the control stick or holding it too tautly; using it as a 'joystick' when its power was no more than equal to that of the rudder or the throttle. Of course, being me, I achieved my

aerobatics, but only after hours of practice. Learning to fly an
aircraft effectively, you need poise, a sense of balance and
utmost mental co-ordination. I was getting quite mischievous
and daring – but always with a necessary coolness in the head
– and I was the only one in my squadron ever to roll a Lysander
. . . before they plucked me out of the sky for the heaven-sent
Henry V.

I looked at all the old Shakespeare films. *The Taming of the
Shrew* – with additional dialogue by Wayne Z. Snooks – contained
little verse. Katharina was played by the world's sweetheart,
Mary Pickford, but it showed Shakespeare's knockabout
rumbustiousness. My performance in *As You Like It* looked
eccentric, the film was excessively 'rural-pictorial', and Rosalind
still crucified the verse with her German accent. But it was
Romeo and Juliet, directed by George Cukor, a man I loved and
a director I admired, which puzzled me most. 'What's wrong?'
I said to myself. 'Norma Shearer and Leslie Howard are fine,
Barrymore is Mercutio, overplaying his mannerisms but not the
part, Basil Rathbone is marvellous as Tybalt and on the screen
his pale blue eyes make him look deadly dangerous. The scenery
and production values are perfectly respectable and first-class:
and yet, it is not succeeding . . .' I felt there was a quarrel
between the eye and the ear, between the behaviour of the
camera and Shakespeare's verse. In the potion scene, for
instance, that 'dismal scene I needs must act alone', the camera
lens was just two inches from Juliet's nose. Shakespeare deliberately gives her a large vocal climax (with even a ghost to shout
at):

> *O, look! methinks I see my cousin's ghost*
> *Seeking out Romeo, that did spit his body*
> *Upon a rapier's point. Stay, Tybalt, stay!*
> *Romeo, I come! this do I drink to thee.*

But, alas, George Cukor shot the scene in the way he'd learnt
to create film climaxes – brilliantly, of course – but he crept the
camera forward, ever so skilfully, to end with a mighty big
close-up. Norma Shearer was so close to the camera she had

to do 'Romeo, I come!' in a whisper to avoid distortion or even laughter of the ribald kind; whereas Shakespeare moves his actress upstage (to a bed with curtains) so that she and the audience can take the strain of a big climax. Time and time again I saw actors who had to come down on the big Shakespeare moments because of the proximity of the camera. More flexibility, poise and balance were needed between Shakespeare's words (and stage directions) and the actions of the camera. Co-ordination.

Big discoveries creep up on you and, later, seem naïve. They swirl out of the mists of half-forgotten words of advice – Hamlet's 'suit the action to the word, the word to the action'. If Shakespeare has a flourish and a big speech, bring the camera back; if he has moments of humour and poignancy, bring it forward. I first tested this out in *Henry V* with an early scene where Henry, on being given the present of tennis balls by the French Dauphin, remarks,

> *We are glad the Dauphin is so pleasant with us; . . .*
> *When we have match'd our rackets to these balls,*
> *We will, in France, by God's grace, play a set*
> *Shall strike his father's crown into the hazard.*

I wanted a big climax on that, so from 'We are glad' (I got a laugh on that) I crept the camera back and back until I stood up suddenly and said 'crown into the hazard' in a full theatrical climax which, to my utmost delight, I saw the camera could take. This was the way to do it. When all the big climaxes come along – 'Once more unto the breach, dear friends' – I was at ease, I didn't have to throttle back. And, what's more, all the other Shakespearean actors, Robert Newton as Pistol included, didn't have to either.

Henry V taught me to love directing on film: taught me to love the medium, taught me how versatile it could be. I'd pull the celluloid through my fingers saying, 'What shall I do with that bit?', holding it up to the light and thinking, how can I get round that mistake? Film taught me to be ingenious, and I learned how to do what the Americans call a Fox-cut. Wonderful expression:

comes from the time when American companies made quota pictures, and the firm that had the worst reputation for doing this was Fox. They used to make these terrible cheap films, then they'd find that they had shot it so badly, that they couldn't cut it. They just couldn't cut back to the love scene or whatever it was, so they would shove in a few lines of inane dialogue to cover up and cut to something irrelevant in between. When a love scene got too broad, they would cut down to the street outside to a kitten rubbing itself against a lamp post.

The most beautiful Fox-cut I ever managed was in *Henry V*. I had shot the whole film and long since taken down the Globe Playhouse when I found myself in trouble. When I put the film together, there was no link to explain at the end how we had got back into the Playhouse again. So I ran the whole film through until I came to 'In your fair minds', turned it round, reversed the action, cut to the long-shot take and then used 'O! for a Muse of fire' and inserted it. Instead of leaving, the actors were now returning. You might think they were walking backwards but they weren't. Marvellous. I am for ever sold on a medium that can do that. Absolute glory.

I enjoyed being the director, I enjoyed being the leading actor. But I didn't enjoy the act of acting a great part on film. I don't think any actor does. I'm always haunted by anxiety, an underlying, constant dread. So, when I say my 'discovery' made me feel at ease acting Shakespeare to the camera (provided it co-ordinates its movements, and angles and lights and shades to my words and actions, sometimes drawing back to a responsive distance to avoid my spitting in its eye), that ease was relative, as it was to all the other Shakespearean actors, too. I was so happy and relieved I'd found a way of lessening an actor's anxiety. On the stage, a tentative actor can hide behind his technique, or the other actors, from which he regains his confidence. On film, a tentative actor looks haunted.

Henry V was a success with the critics and the public. Some said – probably Americans who enjoy celebrating success, enjoy contributing generous praise – it was the best first film since *Citizen Kane*. Servicemen on leave, and ordinary housewives from the Home Front, queued outside the Empire, Leicester

Square, for eleven months. It ran for forty-six weeks in New York. Its opening night was just a few weeks after D-Day. I was so delighted about its success that I would have died a happy man if they'd sent me back flying and my Walrus had blown up. Arthur Rank, who'd gained control of Filippo del Giudice's production company in return for money to finish the film, told me I should have cut the 'unimportant' scenes like Henry's wooing of Katherine – played with delicious humour by Renée Asherson, and part of the delicate balance of the play – and I said 'All right. But the film would have seemed twice as long. I'll show you!' I did, and it did. The film won an Oscar – which did wonders for my prestige, and for my chances of having another go. *Hamlet*, of course.

I soon felt that the film of *Henry V* which had in reality been a marvellous, innovative achievement, was kindergarten, end-of-the-pier stuff: 'Look at this man Shakespeare! He's accessible!' Not quite a film, not quite a play, *Henry V* on screen was a new form of entertainment, an exuberant concoction made (with love) to show that this great playwright could speak to us from the screen.

Now I wanted to try my hand at filming *Hamlet*. I'd played the lead, as I've explained earlier, twice in 1937, in London and at Elsinore; and once you've played Hamlet, the play's thoughts and actions are part of you forever, and so are your thoughts about the play. As I've said before, Hamlet is spectator-proof as well. He fascinates every member of the audience who recognizes – always – something of himself or herself in the dramatic ebb and flow of Hamlet's moods, his inhibiting self-realizations and doubts, his pitiful failure to control events. But I wasn't inhibited in my realization that everyone has his own idea of Hamlet; no, far from it, I was exhilarated.

As Shakespeare's interpreter, I would of course have to be true to his idea of tragedy and make up my mind about the vicious mole in Hamlet's nature. I remembered seeing a Warner Brothers seafaring picture in which Gary Cooper asks an intellectual and sensitive member of the lower deck (Alan Ladd, I think) what book he's reading: '*Hamlet*. A story about a guy who couldn't make up his mind' – which showed that not every

Hollywood scriptwriter was ignorant of Shakespeare, or had little respect for him!

My earliest and deepest resolutions were to find a cinematic interpretation of the play. Emboldened (and slightly chastened) by the popular success of *Henry V*, I didn't initially want to play the part of Hamlet myself. Not because I didn't think I was suited (my stage Hamlet and my stage Romeo – Hamlet's younger brother – had been passionate and successful), but because I didn't want the audience to think, 'Oh, that's just a repeat of Laurence Olivier's Henry V, only this time he's dressed up to look like Hamlet.' That's one of the reasons I gave myself blond hair when I did decide to take the part, for I wished to get well away from the glamorous brunette of a mediaeval king, from my usual image; it was also to make me conspicuous in middle and long shots, not because of any actor-manager conceit, but because Hamlet is always central to the story. The story is seen through his eyes and, when he's not present, through his imagination – his paranoia. This subjective element, paradoxically I think, has encouraged many subjective interpretations over the centuries in many different media: theatre, opera, mime, ballet, and Emlyn Williams's very abridged version for touring before the troops. Much of the verse has been cut out, and even though traditions are handed down, John Gielgud's 1930s Hamlet was quite different from Richard Burbage's original. I thought it quite legitimate to make my own subjective contribution, to make a filmic interpretation to add to the universal consciousness of Hamlet.

If my blond hair was archetypal of the Dane, so much the better; Claudius and Gertrude were dressed as the king and queen of universal playing cards, Hamlet in the timeless doublet and hose of a romantic young prince. The core of Hamlet is his loneliness and desolation after the death of his father, and his feeling of alienation from the new court. In my mind's eye I saw the camera seeing most things through Hamlet's eyes, wandering, or running, through the empty corridors, piercing the vast shadows of Elsinore's great rooms of state for some joy or the sight of some familiar object; but in vain: as lonely as a cloud, with no colour, no silver lining. I was having a flaming row with the Technicolor people at the time – another reason, perhaps, for thinking in black and white – but I would have overcome my sulks if I'd really wanted Technicolor. I liked its subdued colours – greys, sepias and black. But I was terrified by its tangerine and apricot faces, which were not the faces I wished to haunt my melancholy Hamlet.

Black and white had another big, big advantage. I could use deep-focus photography. Deep focus is simply this: the character in the foreground (usually Hamlet) is in focus, so are the characters in the middle ground, and *so* are the characters in the far ground. I say 'simply this': technically it was very difficult – but Desmond Dickinson, my lighting cameraman, was a genius. With deep focus I could beset Hamlet with faces around him which were, to him, too, too solid; I could create distances between characters, giving an effect of alienation, or of yearning for past pleasure as when Hamlet sees Ophelia, in her innocent Victorian dress, an eternity away down the long corridor (150 feet away, actually), sitting on a solid wooden chair – in focus – with love clearly in her eyes. While the camera was showing much of Hamlet's melancholy and the decadence and desolation of Claudius's court, I was able to use the empty spaces for exciting physical action, showing Hamlet's athleticism which is in the play's text – and in my repertoire as an actor, or at least it was. That climax really was tremendous. That fifteen-foot dive, with an open sword, on to Claudius! I first saw the finished version of the film in Australia, and I heard the ladies in the audience go, 'Wow!' And then, of course, the film ends with the dead Hamlet's sad, drum-beat journey up the dark flights of steps and battlements of Elsinore towards his father, the blackness lit by firelight (and, if I may say so, by William Walton's music, which is where my first images of the film began).

Nothing pretty or artificial about the stone of Elsinore; grey, black, sometimes crumbling, sometimes oppressive, sometimes cavernous. At the ends and beginnings of sequences I dissolved the solid flesh of the deep-focus characters away from and into scenes, so that they looked like ghosts. At the beginning of a long walk towards Hamlet, Ophelia looked like a spectre: and it seemed the most natural thing in the world to have Hamlet's soliloquies as words in his head, with his 'To be or not to be' uttered to the sound of a roaring sea, like the sounds which fill the ears of troubled spirits. I once said the film was 'An Essay in *Hamlet*', but that's not quite right. A bit demeaning to the creative impulse which Shakespeare inspired in me and my team; a bit insulting to the resourcefulness of the medium. Why not 'An Interpretation of *Hamlet*'? Or just 'A Film of *Hamlet*'.

Of course, I had to be ruthless in the cutting. Half of *Henry V* went, so did half of *Hamlet*. *Hamlet* is the best-known play in the world. Everyone's got his favourite quotation. I approached the job with terror and the utmost respect, not terror of the purists, but fear that my concept and its execution would be unfaithful to Shakespeare or to the medium; it must be utterly respectful to the spirit of Shakespeare and to the audience's consciousness of Hamlet. I kept bringing the concept sharp into my head so that I knew every second of the length of the film, without a loose moment.

Eileen Herlie, who played Gertrude as a sensual, young middle-aged woman, and I, revelled in the closet scene which, confident of the camera, we played as big as in Drury Lane. All the actors were confident, each gave top-class Shakespearean performances: Jean Simmons as Ophelia, young and sensitive, and Peter Cushing as Osric, one of the best screen actors. Little make-up was worn, and the deep focus showed their confidence – and their sincerity. I used only actors who could speak the verse, either from experience or from their natural talents – like Stanley Holloway, who was the gravedigger. It would be foolish to do a Shakespeare film with actors who'd never been in any of his plays before: he has his own volumes of technique to learn. I rehearsed them before each shot, with a stand-in for me, telling them what I had in mind, telling them the length of each cut, but otherwise giving them their freedom. Restraining them, occasionally, perhaps, but never inhibiting them, and never letting the camera inhibit them. It's not a director's job to teach actors how to act. It's his job to make the most of the talent they already have: to make actors feel relaxed and happy in their work. Of course we missed – those of us who'd known them on the stage – some of the favourite characters, like

Rosencrantz and Guildenstern, who enriched the four-and-a-half-hour pattern of the play which I was changing to the tighter pattern of a two-and-a-half-hour film.

If the shooting has been successful, editing a film is the pinnacle of a director's joy: if not, he must make it so, with no regrets about what exists or does not exist on film, because it's only his joy which will transform the lengths of film and soundtrack into the realization of his imagination. No human mind is big enough to forestall all problems, strong enough to quell the insistence of a last-minute inspiration, but problems in the editing room are usually part of the joy because that's where the medium of film really comes into its own, solving all the difficulties within itself. I was lucky in my editor, Reginald Beck, a consummate technician and a brilliant friend, who saw the point of the camera changing directions in ways hitherto unknown and against the rules, of a character being shot from the left instead of from the right. He realized the drama through Hamlet's eyes and noticed his odd moments of nervous agitation. I was lucky in my composer, my friend William Walton, who absorbed Hamlet's every mood – and mine. We co-ordinated his music and my sound effects: the sound of cannon shots on Hamlet's last journey on the battlements, Hamlet's heartbeat as he sees the ghost of his father for the first time (an effect I borrowed from Jean-Louis Barrault, for which Arthur Rank paid him £500 – which was nothing compared with the royalties he didn't pay to Shakespeare).

The editing room is where the author, medium and audience have their most vital meeting; where the medium – for the others' sakes – must assert its own rhythm, pace and movement and, I suppose, its visual dominance, although it is a big mistake to regard the film as only a visual medium. Shakespeare sometimes poses problems, even to stage directors, with his sudden bursts of 'purple poetry' coming from the most unlikely characters: for instance, the Queen Mab speech from the usually macho Mercutio. So, when Gertrude – sensual and articulate, yes, but hardly poetic, and presumably grief-stricken – describes the drowning of Ophelia by saying 'There is a willow grows askant a brook' followed by some pretty complicated imagery difficult for the modern audience to understand, I thought: 'God, they're going to say to themselves, "Why is she suddenly talking the gobbledegook they talked in the Globe at the beginning of *Henry V?*"' – which would have done Shakespeare no service, either. So I thought: 'Why not let Gertrude speak the lines, but take them away from her visual image, put them in a more universal context? The death of Ophelia, after all, is a vital event in the story. Let it be seen on the screen. Give it full dramatic weight. Reinforce Gertrude's imagery, simplify it, let the audience really see what she is talking about. Clothe the nakedness of her "poetry".' This had to be most delicately edited, and I suffered and enjoyed the dread of doing something new, of being charged with the offence of trying to improve upon Shakespeare's verse. My main aim was clarity. And the result was not tawdry. Another important part of the story is mentioned in a letter from Hamlet, read by Horatio: so I showed Hamlet's sea battle with the pirates – just a glimpse, not too long, but long enough to show his physical courage, and to establish a vital event in the audience's mind.

'How all occasions do inform against me. And spur my dull revenge!' I should quote the soliloquy in full, it is so marvellous; ending with 'O! from this time forth, My thoughts be bloody, or be nothing worth!', which, as I said, I think the most important lines in a play full of important lines. I had the soliloquy in my original concept of the film firmly imprinted on my mind, down to the last second. I shot the Fortinbras bit, which was all right, and the scene with the Fortinbras captain, which was excellent; but during the speech I was wearing a ridiculous tam-o '-shanter hat – designed for me by the otherwise beloved Roger Furse – the edge of which fell over part of my face. I felt uneasy and feared that the audience would wonder why Hamlet was suddenly dressed as another person, away from the shadows of Elsinore, looking at a back-projection seascape, white and glistening – another country. Whether from my unease or a sudden failure of vitality, the speech seemed lifeless – especially flat and stale after the high drama of the way I filmed 'To be or not to be' – and the more I looked at it on the movieola, the flatter it seemed. Murderous to my pride as an actor, murderous to my thoughts about Hamlet, murderous to the text of the play; it had to be cut.

But murder most foul? No! I spared the audience! The tension between text, medium and audience, at this stage, demanded that the story go forward swiftly towards the death of Ophelia from sorrows which did not come singly: first, her father slain; next, Hamlet gone away; next, Laertes returning, speaking revenge, and seeing her final madness. If I'd interrupted this with Hamlet ruminating, debating, discussing, lacerating himself into action, interrupting the action by examining inaction, the audience would have got bored and as irritated by the funny hat as I was.

Hamlet was a success with the public, and with unpedantic critics. I received a Best Actor Oscar, which was good for my career, and wise of the Academy; the Hollywood Establishment had recognized an innovative screen performance which had sprung from one of them – Wyler.

I was not too happy at the way I'd had to cut the final film, for I was a dreamer at heart even if I was also one of Wyler's practical men. Perhaps I'd been too keen on being on budget, on schedule, on being a professional film director. I had succeeded but at a cost. I had ruthlessly cut the volume of Shakespeare's verse. But then in trying to put on film Shakespeare's creative genius, I had no other option.

In the end my verdict on the film of *Hamlet* was a rattling good story, inside and outside Hamlet's mind, told cinematically; and that makes it my favourite Shakespeare film. My acting performance was thrilling enough, but not perhaps as satisfying as Richard III.

I'd made Richard III very much my part in the theatre, and I wanted to make another film. I longed to put Shakespeare, the film director and the film actor together, to bring a classic stage performance to the screen to create a classic film performance. I hoped that I was sufficiently attuned to the part and to the medium as to be able to use the intimacy of the camera to create an even more thrilling and insinuating performance on screen than on the stage. I would woo and charm the audience with my devilish villainy, using close-up and long shot to devastating effect.

Alexander Korda welcomed me with relatively open arms when I took the idea of *Richard III* to him, and I was able to gather my trusted team of Roger Furse, Carmen Dillon and William Walton with Anthony Bushell as associate director. But alas, not Filippo del Giudice, whose soothing presence had seen me through *Henry V* and *Hamlet*. Instead, my new cameraman was Otto Heller.

I'd played Richard III so often on stage, I'd let ham fat grow on my performance. I had to rid myself of this before the cameras got me. So for two weeks I hid myself away and studied the text and my inflections anew, hacked off the extra flesh and the broad gestures I needed on stage to reach the back row of the upper circle some fifty yards away, made myself lean and austere in my expressions, and changed the phrasing, because Richard would be flirting with the camera – sometimes only inches from his eyes – and would lay his head on the camera's bosom if he could. He is the classical actor's favourite bravura part, but he must be kept credible, and the bravura must be carefully marshalled. On the stage his hideous wooing of Lady Anne works brilliantly, but if it's too sudden on the screen the unaccustomed audience would cry, 'Hold. We don't believe this!' So I cut the scene in two, let time pass and gave Richard two glorious climaxes: 'I'll have her; but I will not keep her long', and 'Was ever woman in this humour woo'd?/Was ever woman in this humour won?'

I took Richard's misshapen body and his sardonic smile, but I wanted to convince the audience of the mind behind the mask. A demonic mind, a witty mind. But there's something of the flirting, calculating witch about him, so I kept the long black curls to insinuate this femininity. I made his nose and hump smaller than for the stage, but the nose was big enough to have the effect of concentrating the focus on to the eyes: the only way to the mind when the speech is sardonic or false – unless the mind is dead, like Archie Rice's, which Richard's is not.

Shakespeare's genius fills the play with images of eyes: 'Out of my sight! thou dost affect mine eyes', 'Thine eyes, sweet lady, have infected mine'; of looking glasses, shadows, the sun.

What a gift to the cinema! And what a part to immortalize your acting on the screen! How to pay homage to an acting tradition and to actors over the centuries, including Shakespeare! When an actor gets his eyes right on film he's reached a peak in his professional life. Imagine my joy when Richard is trying to make Buckingham agree to the killing of the Princes in the Tower and I got just the right sort of hatred in his eyes on 'Cousin, thou wast not wont to be so dull:/Shall I be plain? I wish the bastards dead', and on 'Tut, tut! thou art all ice, thy kindness freezes', while cheering up my face. After the shot, for the first time, I didn't have to ask Anthony Bushell, 'How was my expression?' because, for the first time, I was absolutely confident it was what I wanted. The scene ends with Richard turning on Buckingham: 'I am not in the giving vein today.' One of cinema's chilliest moments. The coldness in the eyes was just right. Richard's veins, his mind, were all ice.

I understood the venom in his mind. I felt its mood. Should I say there's a streak of venom in my own nature? No more than the next man. No more than Shakespeare who, by all accounts, led an exemplary life apart from a few default summonses, a writ of libel and some minor disputes over land, which should make us feel even warmer towards him. On the set I was able to treat Claire Bloom, Richard's Lady Anne, with the warm affection I felt for her – constantly – and if, off the set, I sometimes talked to her in Richard's tones, they were insubstantial echoes which made us laugh.

I made a mistake casting Ralph as Buckingham, but he wanted to play him. He wasn't oily enough. There was always a twinkle in his eye. I should have got Orson Welles. Not that he was oily, perhaps the oily aura of medium dry sherry, but he was such a marvellous film man as was seen in his bravura performance in *Citizen Kane*, and its demonic, rule-breaking editing. Welles was a great Shakespearean, his Falstaff in *Chimes at Midnight* is hugely enjoyable, if not a little more demonic in the eyes than Ralph's would have been. Shouldn't there be something of the demon in Buckingham? It was Orson Welles who alarmed the American public by making a spook broadcast about space invaders, which was too real. He would have been admirable.

At the beginning of *Richard III* I let roll the following words –
on an illuminated mediaeval scroll, as we makers of 'historical'
films are wont to do – which I quote in full (for the record):

The Story of England, like that of many another land, is an
interwoven pattern of History and Legend. The History of
the World, like letters without poetry, like flowers without
perfume and thought without imagination, would be a dry
matter indeed without its legends, and many of those, though
scorned by proof a hundred times, seem worth preserving
for their own sake.

I doubt very much if Richard was as evil as Shakespeare makes
out, but the legend Shakespeare creates is so lively it's worth
preserving.

'Now is the winter of our discontent' is the most dramatic
opening speech of any Shakespeare play; a direct, frontal attack
on the audience's sensibilities, more brutal than Richard's upon
Lady Anne's. It's a well-documented tradition of the part that
Edmund Kean leaned his stunted body against the proscenium
arch and mesmerized the audience with his eyes, taking them
into his confidence or alienating them from the action at his will.
What a gift to the cinema Edmund Kean would have been! –
properly directed. On film, I had to get the audience in the mood,
give them some background, before the opening soliloquy. So
I gave them the coronation scene, the last scene from *Henry VI
Part III* (as I had done on the stage of the Old Vic), which has
plenty of mediaeval colour and courtly costumes, and a pompous,
Shakespearean speech from a weak king soon to be overcome
by the cunning and strength of Richard's irony. And there he
was, dressed sparingly in brown and black; a slightly restless
Richard, holding himself apart from the crowd, ridding himself
of his sparse finery to an agitated attendant, glancing anxiously
at the camera to make sure we – the audience – are still
watching. I used a magnificent VistaVision camera which gave
us distinct and solid figures in wide shots, precise and true
features and vivid eyes in its big close-ups. The King and the

others begin to leave, but Richard holds us back with the air of a man anxious to get us alone behind locked doors for a private parley.

Even thinking about the way I shot the soliloquy fills me with pleasure: ideas springing naturally from the text (which, admittedly, I manipulated) and from the main idea of having Richard speak direct to the camera. Ideas which worked because I had the confidence to enact them boldly. The camera goes through the thick wooden door which closes with a firm click behind us – and there is Richard waiting for us, standing next to a small throne at the end of the room. The music of the court continues softly, martial at first, then ending with the lascivious sound of a lute. He briefly pretends to be in a meditative mood, looks at us standing by the door, blinks a modest hesitation, and sways towards us at a commanding pace curtailed a little by the courtesy of a new acquaintanceship and the dragging of his left foot. His disproportion'd gait, his big nose, his stiff black curls add meanness and power to his eyes, whose lids flutter and blink like a gossiping noblewoman's as he stands a foot or so from the camera and speaks to us in clear, crisp tones. For the first seventeen lines of the speech he speaks as though to each one of us personally – you can do that on film – as he explains how he's missed out on the glorious summer of the sun of York because he's not shaped for sportive and amorous tricks. But upon:

> *I, that am curtail'd of this fair proportion,*
> *Cheated of feature by dissembling nature,*

he turns away from the camera to list his deformities (I used ten lines from Act III, Scene II of *Henry VI Part III* for this), to save us embarrassment, perhaps, to gain our sympathy, certainly, to shout a bit, to show his righteous anger. Upon:

> *Why, I, in this weak piping time of peace,*
> *Have no delight to pass away the time,*
> *Unless to spy my shadow in the sun,*
> *And descant on mine own deformity:*

he's standing at the entrance to the large throne room, expecting the camera to come closer to him. So upon 'Then, since this earth affords no joy to me' (the beginning of another five lines from *Henry VI*) he moves towards us,

> *But to command, to check, to o'erbear such*
> *As are of better person than myself,*

and – flatterer – he goes to put his arm around the camera, and we almost feel the gentle touch on our arm, like an importuning uncle's, as we follow him closely towards the big throne room, telling us how he'll make his heaven to dream upon the crown. But we lag behind; so he turns – a little agitated – and puts his arms around our shoulders:

> *And yet I know not how to get the crown,*
> *For many lives stand between me and home.*

Then we follow him as he gets entrapped in that glorious metaphor of 'one lost in a thorny wood', and leave him for his big theatrical climax, standing at the throne:

> *Torment myself to catch the English crown:*
> *And from that torment I will free myself,*
> *Or hew my way out with a bloody axe.*

But he's back at us again, telling us to our face that he can smile, and murder while he smiles, and pushing us back towards the small throne as he lists the way he'll frame his face to all occasions:

> *Can I do this, and cannot get a crown?*
> *Tut! Were it further off, I'll pluck it down!*

He takes a garment from the throne, walks jauntily past us, up some stairs, and leans against a wall near a window. The last thirty lines of his speech were from *Henry VI*. He says to us, after a modest smile: 'Meantime, I'll marry with the Lady Anne.

Here she comes' – we see her through the window – 'Lamenting her lost love.' (Not Shakespeare.) And taking us down a dark passage towards two huge doors which open into the courtyard, he explains who her lost love is:

> *Edward, the Prince of Wales* [my words], *whom I, some*
> *three months since,*
> *Stabb'd in my angry mood at Tewkesbury.*
> *A sweeter and a lovelier gentleman . . .*
> *The spacious world cannot again afford . . .*
> *And made her widow to a woeful bed.*
> *(Richard III*, Act I, Scene II)
> That from his loins no hopeful branch may spring,
> To cross me from the golden time I look for!
> *(Henry VI, Part III*, Act III, Scene II)

. . . and he pushes the doors open. We see Lady Anne walking behind her husband's coffin, and the circle on the top right-hand corner of the screen which tells the projectionist the reel of film is about to finish.

It's very bad practice to have a reel-break in a dramatic scene: a sleepy projectionist can ruin everything. Most film processes have ten-minute reels, but VistaVision, because of its technique for producing such clear images, only had five, so throughout the soliloquy I was aware of a shortage of time, and that gave the performance an extra edge. Ah! Sweet problems of film that add to the dread and the adrenalin of acting! No doubt to the horror of school teachers, and the confoundment of their pupils, I left out the lines:

> *And therefore, since I cannot prove a lover,*
> *To entertain these fair well-spoken days,*
> *I am determined to prove a villain.*

because I simply don't believe them. Even Shakespeare makes him a 'credible' lover. Improving on Shakespeare? Sacrilege? The part was the thing. Within his own extraordinary world I had to keep Richard credible, and film audiences are the most difficult to convince. Besides, I had difficulty saying the lines. They didn't seem real to me, and might have affected the brilliance of the rest.

Richard talks and nods and winks to us while things are going well for him: and if he doesn't lean against the proscenium exactly, he leans against the half-open shutter of a window, giving a commentary on the politics of the court below, a report on the success of his plotting. He's very self-conscious about his clothes, and, after the successful wooing of Lady Anne, he's so pleased with himself he barely notices us, and talks to himself and the sun:

> *Shine out, fair sun, till I have bought a [looking] glass,*
> *That I may see my shadow as I pass.*

He changes brown and black with blue accessories (blue is for boy, but his had feminine tones), to an elaborate deep red costume, with white lace and the white figure of a hog stamped on each glove. But back to the plain garb when he says his prayers with the bishops, and swings down the bell rope to call back the citizens of London to proclaim him king. But when he's king, he behaves badly and has to go to battle, his long hair looking incongruous and ugly in his black mediaeval armour; and he's no longer talking to us because troubles and ghosts have come betwixt us and him. He'll have to offer more than his kingdom to get horse and sympathy from us.

'Here pitch our tent, even here in Bosworth field' – curses to Richard for that. We shot the battle scene in Spain, and those stunted Spanish trees and the silver grass were not Bosworth. When Richard insisted on a view of his battlefield, I was forced to use a painted picture of Leicestershire with the trees a little less stunted. Who has the faintest idea what Bosworth field looks like except people who live near Bosworth, and they're not mediaeval?

I was injured at Bosworth, as I was in the other Shakespeare films. I was in the battle on a horse, padded with cork. I got a technician to fire an arrow into the padding over the horse's body (I'd pull the horse up, someone would unsettle its back legs, and thus the horse would fall in battle), but his arrow missed the padding and went into my leg.

'Impossible!' the stubborn English technician said, several times, in the Spanish sun.

'Pull the arrow out and see my blood on the end of it,' I said.

He did. 'I still don't believe it,' he said, absolutely aghast that his craft went wrong. Not so worried about my wound.

The film got several awards for its craft and technique. *Richard* was nominated for an Oscar, but lost to another King – Yul Brynner. It lost money the first time round, was revived successfully in 1966, is now enjoying a fresh release in the cinema with a new print and, who knows, in a hundred years' time it may be a cult cassette. But the film's initial flop made it impossible for me to get the money to make *Macbeth* – in my mind a director's film (I've found him to be a difficult acting part), a blood-coloured, murky picture. And the British craftspersons now working brilliantly on Star Wars pictures would have helped me create an absolutely real and believable supernatural world: the lizard's legs and the poisoned entrails Hecate's witches throw into the hell-broth would be horrifyingly real. I could have taken stalwart Scottish actors, like John Laurie and Andrew Cruickshank, to Scotland to sup full of the horrors of the blasted heath or, if the budget were small, to Yorkshire, where *Wuthering Heights* should have been filmed. But, no money, no budget. One may be daring, bold and resolute, even a bloody dreamer, but one cannot laugh to scorn the power of money men. So posterity is dispossessed of another version of the Scottish play to compare with Orson Welles's or Roman Polanski's.

SIXTEEN

IN FRONT OF THE CAMERA

I have always been an actor who moulds characteristics to hide my personality. I take parts of the character *into* myself – not on to, otherwise they'd fall off. I do not search the character for parts that are already in me, but go out and find the real personality I feel the author created. I work all this out before I begin to rehearse the part and build the role up from within, knowing that the camera will expose me if I am not true, if my imagination is askew or only at half power; if I am doing anything unreal. I make use of my natural talents and make sure that I do not waste other people's time on the set.

After the grimness of *Richard III* and my disappointment over *Macbeth*, I thought it would be fun to work with the legendary beauty and comedy actress Marilyn Monroe as both her leading man and her director, but I had not bargained with the problems of 'method' acting.

I went to one of Lee Strasberg's New York classes once and saw him bullying a boy who I saw had a good feel for character. 'He's got so many faults,' Lee said, and went off into a lot of hot air, sprinkled with clichés. 'The only fault he's got is the confidence you are draining from him,' I said, or words, I hope, to that effect. Probably more pompous because I was angry. No doubt Strasberg thought English actors knew nothing of Stanislavsky, but we had all read him avidly when his books came out. Some of us – misunderstanding him – even used to come in an hour earlier and smell the furniture on the set. He was no high-falutin' phoney, he was an intensely practical man in the Wyler mould. By all means have Stanislavsky with you in your study or in your limousine or wherever you are three hours before the scene, but don't bring him on to the film set, where the schedule is tight and the time is ripe for fizzing action to carry along the story.

My feathers were considerably ruffled by Marilyn's erratic behaviour on and around the set; her spikiness and spite were frightening, split from her sweetness and vulnerability. Half the time her head was so full of the rigmarole of 'method', her natural talent was suppressed. She'd take ages over a shot, keep people waiting for hours. 'Marilyn, I've got the whole film in my head and this shot's fifty seconds long. You've got to make it thirty-eight seconds shorter . . .' However, she could be a dream, listening and understanding my idea of a scene, taking off-camera directions beautifully, and proving her physical beauty and comic timing to be historical facts.

At one point, when Marilyn had to talk in a silly, drunken way, I told her to get on with the scene and not take the slightest bit of notice of what I did or said. Then I began to embroider round her, talking at the same time; an idea the Lunts invented in the 1920s. The audience can hear the bits they need to know, but the effect is killingly funny and can be magical. Difficult to do, though.

I had been amused by Terence Rattigan's original script for *The Sleeping Princess* on the stage, but found it hard to love the character in the film version which the money men had christened *The Prince and the Showgirl*, making it sound like an Edwardian musical. As the Prince, I needed something real to grasp on to (the man *was* odious), so I based the accent on Alexander Korda's (though he wasn't), and some of the mannerisms, including a lot of fun with an eyeglass (I was so confident with my eyes!), on King Paul of Greece, whom I had watched behave badly and unprofessionally at a reception – something minor Royalty is prone to do, I believe. In the editing room I had a happier time than I expected. I loved cutting away to Marilyn's reaction shots; no one had such a look of hurt innocence or of unconscious wisdom, and her personality was strong on the screen. She gave a star performance.

I was fifty. What a happy memory it would have been if Marilyn had made me feel twenty years younger, but I was upset by her insolence, which showed my age, I suppose. Still my theatre work and my film work with people like Wyler had taught me discipline and a respect for experience. I was usually directing fellow actors who felt the same, telling them what I wanted, letting them do what they wanted as far as I could, solving technical problems by discussion and by drawing upon experience. One of the glories of working in the theatre or in films is the teamwork, the trust; the cool trust needed to overcome the otherwise superhuman task of realizing the imagination. Maybe I was tetchy with Marilyn and with myself, because I felt my career was in a rut.

It did not remain so for long. The 1950s saw a major change for me. As I have explained earlier, John Osborne introduced me to the world of the young modern writer through Archie Rice with his seedy bowler hat, his tatty bow tie and dingy check jacket.

In some ways it was not as difficult for me to make this change as it was for more mannered, effusive actors, for those who built their characters round themselves. My acting had always had contemporary characteristics: it had always been inventive and as spontaneous as possible. I had always tried to be a real person. (But not at the expense of verse, of course; if it was Shakespeare, I would find reality *through* the verse.) To me spontaneity meant talking as people do in everyday conversation. I hardly ever say a full sentence without at least four 'ummms' and an 'aaah', and I often pause for a time to find the right word. That's very much part of a natural performance for me: I would call that actual spontaneity. After I have produced my final performance by a process of selection made during my full-out rehearsals, I add spontaneity: the cherry in the cocktail. It is hard to achieve, so I always put it in last. In a long run you have to reproduce technical spontaneity over and over again and make it real every night. On film you have to keep it diamond sharp and never go over the top.

Film acting taught me to have sincere eyes on stage. There's no point in exaggerating your eyes in the theatre because they only reach the first five rows of the stalls anyway, and there's a danger they'll become detached and flash to and fro across the footlights like coiled china eyes worn by clowns at children's parties. Archie Rice had to have flashing music-hall eyes, which were dead underneath, and we achieved that much better on film. (Full circle from the passion I finally achieved in Heathcliff's eyes by ridding myself of the habits of the stage.) As with Richard III, the camera relished the intimate parts of Archie – and John Osborne wrote some more scenes to give the film of *The Entertainer* what it wanted, craved: more emotion. I think the film allowed John to show more of Archie Rice. I tuned up my stage performance, often changed it. I looked to the subtlety, the expressiveness, the reality of his mannerisms and accent (based on music-hall chums I'd lived with in theatrical digs, and artistes I'd seen in my youth), rehearsed the cheap music-hall flickers and flutters for the surfaces of the eyes, and made him dance expressively (at almost full theatrical throttle) and badly – which I achieved by dancing as well as I could! And the camera caught the deadness behind the eyes. Archie Rice was a hollow man. We are the hollow men. I felt Archie's hollow mood because that's what the camera wanted. Or was I feeling middle-age disillusion at the time? I am not a hollow man, but I know what it feels like to be one!

We all acted well in that picture, and Tony Richardson, the director, made the most of us and the medium. Joan Plowright revealed the clear and honest eyes of a true film actress. (Am I not to be allowed a tribute to my wife?) Alan Bates, Albert Finney, Daniel Massey, Shirley Anne Field, Charles Gray, Miriam Karlin and Joan joined us older actors, Brenda de Banzie and Roger Livesey, with Thora Hird flitting delightfully, as ever, between; and all of us, and the music-hall acts, presented a pretty lively picture of mid-century blues. For the first and last time I was able to cry tears on the screen, in the scene when Archie hears that his son's all right as his mistress is washing after fornication. I don't quite know how it happened. Relief at the news of the son. Maybe the challenge that a cheap music-hall artist would have the versatility to cry to order.

John Osborne's *The Entertainer* lifted my spirits to new heights. I was no longer in a rut; I immensely enjoyed the challenge of the new, the chance to adapt my knowledge and abilities into fresh channels. Details of all the films I have made since Archie Rice are in my autobiography. I cannot discuss them all again here. I will just comment on a few aspects of some of them which I remember particularly well and which may be of interest.

I enjoyed my supporting roles in modern films. As usual I put all I could into the parts – undemanding though they were in many ways, for an actor who had played kings and princes – determined always to appear convincing. I was particularly amused by the dry irony of Shaw's Burgoyne in *The Devil's Disciple*; there's no harm in an audience seeing an actor enjoying himself. Here again I was able to use my eyes to great effect and play the ironic, civilized soldier to the top of my bent. For Crassus in *Spartacus*, I was passing through a patrician phase, but I gave him a touch of that flirting femininity of Richard III, the cool eyes, suddenly aflame – second cousin to Coriolanus, several times removed.

Several theatre productions of mine were made into films, including *Uncle Vanya*, a play with which I had great success at the Chichester Festival Theatre; and *The Three Sisters*, based on a beautiful production from the National with a marvellous cast. It was a celebration of the acting rather than a thoroughly conceived filmic version of the play. That would have been a mammoth task for which we had neither time nor money.

I had a couple of 'visual' sequences, such as Irina's dream of a better future in Moscow, and the camera seemed to like Chekhov's dialogue and his shifts of mood. I had little to do with the screenplay, which made it not-a-director's film in my book. All encouragement to the film man who will tackle Chekhov wholeheartedly. He could have much reward. Too wordy, maybe, but I've a feeling that as we go further into high tech, cassettes and private entertainment, people will have a yearning for more words. Especially if conversation dies.

But films based on obvious stage origins sometimes misfire. Stuart Burge directed the film of the National's *Othello*, and he did it marvellously, within its limited concept. Alas, my performance was tired. I mistimed effects. Somehow I was lacking in confidence and full vitality; perhaps, subconsciously, I was being gnawed by the question: 'Why aren't we making a full-blown Shakespeare film of this?' Certainly I regret that now.

Immediately after *Othello*, I played the Mahdi in *Khartoum*, with Charlton Heston playing Gordon. His 7 feet down to my 5 feet. A consummate actor who (it is said, and I happily concede) acted me off the screen – not from want of trying on my part. Making up as the Mahdi, I put white greasepaint along the lower edge of each eye to increase its size, as I had done for both the play and the film of *Othello*.

'Oh no, oh no, don't do that, black is what you want,' they all said.

'Won't it make my eyes look tiny?'

But they were right. I kicked myself for not having discovered this before. Black on the edge and quite a lot of black round the eye is far more effective; it made me look much more African.

When making *Khartoum*, I was relaxing after *Othello*, recharging my spirits and my bank account, prepared to experiment a bit with the effects I'd learnt from *Othello* but on a less demanding level. This is not putting the part of the Mahdi down. Tony Guthrie told me not to. But in epic pictures there's not much time for deep characterization – sometimes the dialogue can be anybody's – and you have to rely very strongly on the pictorial effect. Every epic film has its flamboyant part – usually played by Peter Ustinov. The secret is to play the part up to the audience's expectation of it – a healthy tradition from Shakespeare to Westerns and Mae West – and the real amusement is the little extra. A great deal more extra, if it's real. We all loved Charles Laughton for his big performances. It's given me a lot of fun being part of that cinema tradition.

And I'm not diffident about playing the ordinary man again, as I did with Simone Signoret and Sarah Miles in *Term of Trial*. Not boring myself. Getting closer to myself, perhaps. Not boring the audience. And learning all the time. Franklin Schaffner, who directed *Nicholas and Alexandra*, was having a bit of a go at Michael Jayston, who played Nicholas: 'Make him weaker!' So Michael, one of our finest young actors, tried to make him weaker, but it just looked like weak acting. Then we noticed his eyes watered when he acted anger – just something he could do, lucky man, a marvellous natural gift. You can hardly do better than that as a symbol of weakness. Show the camera his eyes. I played rather a little man in *Bunny Lake is Missing*, probably bullied on to me by Otto Preminger – a real bully, who never stopped. Noël Coward and I didn't like the man much. Almost put me off his *Carmen Jones*, which I thought an inspired piece of work. I have a taste for mixing forms, for experiment, and *Carmen Jones* was an innovative film. It's a miracle it came from such a heavy-handed egotist. Have a pleasant atmosphere on the set and a director is in less need of a miracle.

I found *The Dance of Death* by Strindberg a pretty claustro-phobic piece in which you can't open out too much, unlike *Miss Julie*. Strindberg is *veritas*, perfectly straightforward, no undercurrent, no sub-text, no sneaky underneath thought that he is either subconsciously unaware of or is hiding to himself. Quite unlike his fellow Scandinavian Ibsen, who has a subtext of pure filth and a very strong undercurrent which can have an extremely bad effect on the actor. The sub-text is so dirty, really; well, if not dirty, then salacious. The part of Strindberg's Edgar is a big one – intense and emotional – and that's how I played it on the screen, daring and risky; and if occasionally I appeared to go over the top, that didn't ruin the performance or discount the screen's potential to contain a big performance. You have to follow the rhythms, the death-dance rhythms of the play. My feelings for the part were right. My intentions for the film were right. I swam along with the other actors, especially Geraldine McEwan, my leading lady. Any flaws, put down to professional misjudgement in a profession where the watchword should not be caution.

The physical disorders which, at times, drained me of vitality started in the mid–1960s. Cancer when I was sixty. Actors, like other devout professionals, don't like talking about their diseases. (If a man has a memorable professional achievement it's very likely he'll forget – if he knows – the spur his illness gave him, or whatever the upheaval was.) If you haven't the vitality, don't act. If you can't do it, don't do it. An actor must be constantly vigilant about his energy, even when he's young and he thinks his body can take every abuse. The body is a vital part of the equipment. I used to keep very fit – best for the movement, the gestures – and only a few years before the cancer I'd reached a peak in a Stratford *Coriolanus*, appearing heroically half-clothed without any feeling of unease. The vitality doesn't disappear altogether, of course; that would be the end of life. You have to nurse it.

I had to do cameo roles for the sake of my health, the balance of my professional life, the balance of my social life – and my bank account. Working with friends. Working for friends. I did a sort of double act with Frank Finlay in that film where my friend Anthony Quinn wears *The Shoes of the Fisherman*. (Brave man, Frank Finlay. He had a very shaky start with Iago on the stage, but he persevered, and ended by giving the best performance in the film.) Richard Attenborough asked me to do Field-Marshal French in his brilliant directing début *Oh! What a Lovely War*, which was a bright couple of days in Brighton – which might have been the trouble with the film, where the songs didn't have the same eerie effect that they had in the theatre. Richard and I did another double act, Mr Creakle and Mr Tungay, in an American television version of *David Copperfield* which wasn't made with as much love and humour as George Cukor's 1934 film. A magnificent British cast, though. No cameo parts in Dickens, they're all gems. Cameos are sparkling gems set in strong relief against a subdued background. Film producers put them into their epics to ensure some sharpness, bitterness, humour – flash some money on a bit of class. They ensure an actor an income and an opportunity to meet old friends. I always chose interesting parts and usually had the chance to be relatively relaxed, to be the larger-than-life character audiences want, and have wanted, since pantomime, music hall and early film Westerns. Vital to me, these cameos – spiritually and financially. I've always managed to give them all the animation they need.

Time, strength and the opportunity to do a full-length film part arrived with *Sleuth* – an amusing script by Anthony Shaffer, from his stage play. Very clever, if a little repetitious, like his brother Peter, who has gone on and on repeating his stage successes on film: I understand *Amadeus* is a veritable feast of colour and music, impossible to achieve on stage. I suppose I've reached an age when I can see the massive further potential of the cinema – well, film in its broadest sense – and when I can wholeheartedly admire other people's contributions to its development, feel pleased about my own, but feel regret at what I didn't achieve or do, even for my own pleasure.

The making of *Sleuth* was, for me, tinged with nostalgia and hope for the future. The part was big and good enough to test my powers to amuse on a sustained level. Joseph Mankiewicz, its director, has always been concerned with words on the screen – a wordsmith, a screensmith. He made *All About Eve*, with its witty dialogue and voice-overs; a very fine screen version of Shakespeare's *Julius Caesar* with brilliant performances by Marlon Brando as Antony and John Gielgud as Cassius (not so different in style as they may seem); and *Guys and Dolls*, with most of the lyrics kept intact – a film which broadened the public's consciousness of the American stage musical and, no doubt, contributed to my wish to do a stage production at the National, in which I would play Nathan Detroit as well as Frank Sinatra did (but differently), and dance as well as Archie Rice, and sing like Macheath in *The Beggar's Opera*. Michael Caine was an absolute delight in *Sleuth* (except he didn't like rehearsing – I went through my lines with the continuity girl). The camera loves him just as much as we who work with him do. I can see him in the Gary Cooper role in *High Noon* – but with his Cockney charm the townsfolk would all have been his deputies by 11.30 a.m. No! His professional discipline is too powerful for that. He has the true personality of a star, and in *Sleuth* – in particular the scene on the staircase – he showed deep and difficult emotion. He's restless to widen his range. Mark my words. The mark of Caine on the cinema will be deeper yet.

Michael Caine is, in fact, young enough to be my son. For the last ten years I've worked in films with technicians and

actors who are a generation or so behind me – or in advance of
me, if you look at the ways of professional leadership (I've
provided the example), and finding fresh ideas for and from the
medium. It warms my heart to see young people – any people
– expressing their talents. I've had a family, and I've wanted to
help them do what they want to do in life. I've wanted to be a
contented family man. I've never been a star who gets paid a
million dollars a picture; and when I was a dashing young stage
actor or a Hollywood star, or a stage and film director, a theatre
administrator, when I was acting classical roles, I didn't set up
educational trusts for my children, and when you are ill you
become very anxious for your wife and family.

Actually, I was pleased with the parts I played – not wholly
for the money – in films like John Schlesinger's *Marathon
Man* (particularly good), *The Boys from Brazil* (interesting and
heartening seeing Gregory Peck play an unsympathetic part)
and, yes, even *The Betsy*. They were usually shot in exotic
places, or the sun shone and life was relatively easy. They were
all rattling good 'entertainment' pictures, expertly made, with
touches of the innovative. The parts I played were lively and
expertly done, which is amusing in itself, both for me and for
the audience. I can't go along with the critics who say I lowered
myself playing these parts. On no account should a critic know
of an actor's domestic and physical problems, but I wish he (or
she) would be more aware of the so-called classical actor's need
for his enjoyments – like Graham Greene's 'entertainments', or
Shakespeare's, Chaucer's, T. S. Eliot's (who would have given
him a cat's chance of being a hit on Broadway? Didn't he get a
Tony Award for the best lyrics?).

An actor's entertainments refresh him, reach other parts, get
him tuned up for the arduous classical roles. It's an English
tradition for the highbrow to feed on the vulgar, to be subsidized
by light relief – English eclecticism. Get a New York 'method'
actor to say that! Get a New York snooty film critic to think
that! Not that I'm snooty about film critics as I used to be snooty
about films. I regard the best of them as partners. We love the
medium. We enjoy making new discoveries together. Critics
like Dilys Powell, and most of the modern-day ones. Every

actor, workaday, classical, needs his critics. Early days for the film yet. Early days for the film actor. Early days for the film critic. I hope we keep up with each other and keep away from the high-falutin' cant which has sometimes affected the stage.

Fundamentally, I think, television is a more 'hearing' and 'listening to' medium than the cinema, where the picture is bigger and the eyes can wander only to darkness. So you can use more words, more details in characterization, you can give a more intimate performance. Startling effects are permissible if you've got the audience in the mood for them. You can sustain emotional effects for long periods, with relatively bare settings, as the Royal Shakespeare Company did with their studio *Macbeth* with Ian McKellen and Judi Dench.

I had the marvellous opportunity of doing a number of well-known plays for Granada Television: Pinter's *The Collection* (those Pinter pauses on the TV screen are fascinating), *Cat On A Hot Tin Roof, Come Back Little Sheba*: I found that the medium can take any play, any performance, provided – yes, back to it! – the feeling is right. I can do anything if I am prepared. I can look the littlest man in the world if I am *ready*. I could play so little, you wouldn't recognize me. But it takes time. Get your integrity together and you'll integrate with the medium.

I always go to endless trouble to learn American accents, even for small television parts. If it's north Michigan, it's bloody well got to be north Michigan. If it's Kansas, it's goddam well got to be Kansas. I go to endless trouble to find someone to teach me. Because you learn to say the lines with an inflexion that a local person would use automatically from birth, that doesn't mean you are not playing the part. The teacher is not teaching me how to act. Of course there were times when I said to the teacher: 'I know that isn't quite right but I feel I need a variety of tonal touches in that scene so I hope you won't mind if I say it a little wrongly. Sometimes tonal values are more important to a scene than a perfect accent. The audience'll have a helluva lot of perfect accents but I hope I will have won their trust by that scene. If I haven't won them over by then, I never will.'

When I wanted a Mississippi accent for *Cat on a Hot Tin Roof*, I couldn't find a single soul at the American Embassy in London who could cough me up one. The nearest was a nineteen-year-old girl from Tennessee. It worried me that she wasn't very Mississippi. Of course she'd already begun to ape the English accent and there are very few nineteen-year-olds who have what it takes to tell me what to do and how to do it, so I was very worried. Maureen Stapleton and the director kept saying I was fine but I wondered whether it was Mississippi enough.

My fellow National Theatre actors and I successfully brought our stage performances of *The Merchant of Venice* and *Long Day's Journey into Night* to the television screen – successful, but not conceived as television performances. Of course, there have to be adjustments – my false teeth for Shylock were slightly smaller – but the barriers are down. English eclecticism, Wyler's 'do all that can be done', are thriving. Film – in its widest sense – is indeed a great medium. I'm just sorry I stood aloof from television film for so long.

Maybe I haven't said enough about the technique of film acting. The technique of film direction, yes, perhaps. I've talked about making an actor feel at ease. Take a cricketer. The groundsman gives him a perfect wicket. The bowler gives him the perfect ball, and he executes a beautiful cover drive which gets him four runs and has the spectators on their feet. Ask him how he does it, and he'll explain that his back-lift was short (miraculously so) and his bat straight.

'But how do you make it so sweet and beautiful?'

'I don't know. All I can tell you is it feels good.' The steps leading up to a spectacular shot like a hook shot may be easier to explain; but why does a batsman do a hook shot when he could so easily be caught out rather than make a six? Showing off? Testing his repertoire? Giving the spectators a thrill?

And John McEnroe. He's got a beautiful backhand. But at the Wimbledon Celebration Ball, what's his dancing like? I bet, with a few lessons, he'd be closer to *Come Dancing* than ever Archie Rice would be. You can't teach a man rhythm if he hasn't got it. McEnroe's serve, I understand, wasn't as strong as usual when he fell in love with a beautiful actress. Perhaps he should have taken a million dollars, taken a year off and given vent to his versatility, and so saved his game. 'There's nothing wrong with my game!' Yes, of course: how can I possibly say? He may have shown signs of feeling a little out of sorts with his game. He could hardly blame his 'technique', as though it was an independent wilful creature. When I see an actor like Michael Caine, who's never out of sorts with the camera or the world, give a performance of natural feeling and power without any apparent technique, I wonder if technique should be given any independent identity. Mind you, I'm almost as 'natural' as Michael is. I'm naturally more of a show-off than he is. I'm more versatile – as yet! I have more technique!

I do wish we'd see more actors of Marlon Brando's calibre on television. More classically-trained stage actors should appear regularly on the box, explore its possibilities like I explored film's, and create classical television roles. John Mortimer's father in *Voyage Round My Father* is a classical television role in the sense that future actors will want to play it, and will, specifically on television. Try to forget its so-called stage origins. John wrote it from his mind and soul, with love and knowledge of his father, and with love and knowledge of the medium of television. Some critic or other said I played the old man as though rehearsing my own old age – something absurd like that. Was I rehearsing my own death as Lord Marchmain in *Brideshead Revisited* (if so, it's going to be a most giggly, light-hearted affair)? My own madness and death in *King Lear*? Lear, of course, is a classical stage role; it needs the resonance of the theatre. But you can capture the intimate very well on television; the fond, foolish old man. Doing *Lear* on television was an exercise of will for me, with a great deal of help from my friends, especially Michael Elliott, the director, alas now dead. The will to get the right vitality and reality. Physically it was arduous. My frailty suited the old man. I suppose I felt his mood. Loved him. I felt the mood of all my old men.

My wife, Joan, threatened to feed me nothing but bread and dripping and to have Otto Preminger as a house guest if I ended my acting career at the National by doing *Lear*. Happily, I did

The Party instead. (Incidentally, Trevor Griffiths also writes
very well for television.) As it turns out, Lear is to be my last
major role, on stage or screen. But, if you'll excuse a bit of
sentimental fancy, *The Tempest* was Shakespeare's acknowledged last play and, reputedly, Prospero was Richard Burbage's
last role. As Prospero's charms are all o'erthrown and what
strength he has is his own, and as he prepares to leave his
magical island, Shakespeare has him say:

> *Our revels now are ended. These our actors,*
> *As I foretold you, were all spirits and*
> *Are melted into air, into thin air:*

and I think film has proved him wrong.

Just a moment or two of nostalgia. I'm happy, witty, wise and
unpretentious, especially when I'm with friends like George
Cukor and Katharine Hepburn, whom I was with for the American television production of *Love Among the Ruins*. (Actually,
George was very good at pretending to be pretentious.) That
was my happiest professional film experience. Master and mistress of the medium, and it must have shown in our performances. With Hepburn – as with all the great stars – you have a
deep sense of her personality, of her strong and still centre of
gravity which radiates her wit, her vulnerability, her courage
and her outspokenness, like Shakespeare's verse radiates his
Rosalind in *As You Like It*. I could never aspire to Hepburn's
star quality, I didn't have Cukor's knowledge of technique or his
great knack with screen actors, but we felt equal and comfortable
in our shared love for the medium. All actors are egotistical and
competitive – that's where we get our energy. It's our love of
the art of acting (and its camaraderie) which makes us artists.
You can feel the vitality in the performances of Hepburn and
Richardson, for example, in *Long Day's Journey into Night* –
superb examples of ensemble playing and film acting.

Ralph Richardson, John Gielgud and I competed with each
other in those scenes when we were all together in Tony
Palmer's marathon *Wagner* – there was very little else to do.
So often the case when you're blockbustering. We certainly

competed in the classical stage roles. Do you know the most affecting thing about my 'affair' with Richard III? John Gielgud passed on to me the sword Edmund Kean had used in his performance. A great and unselfish and typical act of friendship, but a greater act of love for the art of acting. Actors' camaraderie stretches back to Shakespeare, at least, and it must continue. The stage will be all right, with varying degrees of flourishing. But you might have to form a television repertory company.

As the centre of gravity of my body moves closer to its grave and my soul thinks of Heaven, I'm expected to show a touch of *gravitas*, to give advice. I would be appalled if I met a modern film actor who didn't love his medium – snooty now as I was snooty then. The wonder of Willie Wyler's medium and the reality of his predictions are everywhere to be seen; television is showing the medium's growth and history. Film will go anywhere you want to take it. If I'd been born ten years earlier, say, in Hollywood, I wonder if I would have found my way to words, Shakespeare, the stage and the classical roles. Certainly I'm prejudiced to say 'get a classical training', but you must act as the spirit moves you. (Work on a building site rather than go to a 'method' studio.)

If you love your art and your medium, what can be added to Tony Guthrie's 'Love the character you play'? If you're having trouble with your relationship with the camera, look to your make-up, gestures and expressions; look to your eyes; look to within yourself. And get your feeling and mood right. If all else fails, talk to the director!

Unlike the fading Prospero in Shakespeare's final Epilogue, you lack neither spirits to enforce nor art to enchant.

PART FIVE

REFLECTIONS

SEVENTEEN

ON ACTING

Acting is like the first sip of beer, the one you probably steal as a child, the taste that you never forget, it makes such an impression on your palate. No other sip ever tastes the same, always just a little different. Acting is often put down by outsiders, who are not interested anyway, as a game played by adults who ought to know better. It is not; it is a great art and, when it is done well, it stands out on its own, supreme and satisfying.

Mind you, the same Philistines who call us children in long trousers would more than likely find a Turner painting not much to look at – 'Those shadows are purple, aren't they?' – and a Van Gogh a botch of colours that doesn't compare with their children's kindergarten finger-paintings. These zombies who occupy the same planet as us would think Beethoven a painful cacophony, Bach a Welsh choirmaster, and Chopin something you do when you split wood for the fire.

I have been acting all my adult life – and before. It has stood by me and I have stood by it. It has given me much joy and some sorrow. It has taken me to places that otherwise I would not have seen. It has given me the world and great happiness. It has brought me friends and good companionship, camaraderie and brotherliness. It has taught me self-discipline and given me the retentive eye of an observer. It has enabled me to love my fellow men. It has clothed me, watered me, fed me, and kept me away from a bowler hat and a nine-till-five desk. It has given me cars, houses and holidays, bright days and cloudy ones. It has introduced me to kings and queens, presidents and princes. It has no barriers; it has no class. Whatever your background, if it decides to embrace and take you to its heart, it will hurl you up there amongst the gods. It will change your wooden clogs overnight and replace them with glass slippers.

I have been lucky, I admit – nay, boast – for I have been successful for most of my working life. But the wonderful thing about this business is that it can thrust accolades on you at any moment, at any time. It is never too late. At eighty, when you are about to suck in your final breath, it can turn you into a star. It is always just around the corner.

Once you have been to the tree and tasted the fruits, some sour, some sweet, you will never be able to leave it alone again. It will get under your nails and into your pores, it will mix with your blood, and nothing will ever take it away from you. It has its ups and downs, twists and turns, great fortune and bad luck. It has its own superstitions and its own language. It has its 'in' crowds and its 'out' crowds, its jealousies and its loves. It can destroy you in all sorts of canny ways with drink, drugs, success or failure. It can change charming personalities into monsters, and big egos into even bigger ones. It can make you believe your own publicity. It can make you sit on your behind and feed on past glories. It can leave you in a pile of yesterday's press cuttings and laugh at you as you wonder what happened to your real self. It is selective and very surprising. It can make you give up everything else. It will blinker you to personal relationships and destroy marriages and families. It can turn even twins against each other. It can rape you, bugger you, bless you and succour you. Its moods change with the wind. Once you have made your decision, if you believe enough, there is positively no turning back. Above all, you must remain open and fresh and alive to any new ideas.

It's all very well having a head full of the past, we can all sit in bed and dream our dreams of yesterday. I'm sure I could fill a waking day without moving from the bedroom. But that's not important, that's merely cosy and comforting like a child's blanket. What is important is tomorrow. You must never let that

slip out of sight. Hold on to it strong and fast. Keep it firmly
fixed inside you, so that you are looking ahead at all times.
Reminisce by all means, talk of the past as I have, but always
keep your sights fixed firmly on the future; otherwise, you may
as well stop now, at this very moment. Stop and bury your toes
in yesterday's concrete.

I have always been fascinated by the theatre in all its aspects.
I like to know how every nut and bolt fits together. I've
attempted to learn every little detail. I've always believed that
you can't ask a man to do something unless you've been there
yourself. So I made a point very early on of understanding how
a theatre breathes. Believe me, when you are second assistant
stage manager at eighteen for Sybil Thorndike's company, you
learn very quickly.

I learned, too, very early on from Noël Coward. In *Private
Lives*, Adrienne Allen and I were obviously mere feeds to the
glorious Gertie Lawrence and the great Noël. Not that there is
anything wrong in this at the beginning, but it really is most
frustrating when you are desperate for a part of the apple to
bite. Noël, of course, was the author and admitted in all honesty
that his own part and Gertie's could be equally well played
without any other characters in the play. Charming! But I knew
that beneath all that bravado, they both needed us as the
tinderbox is needed to fire off the rocket. I only mention this
because it is a state of growing in our business. I knew that to
be fed well, your feed had to be perfect. And that the better
you feed, the more likely one day you will be fed. Early days
. . . but never to be forgotten. Lessons, blackboard, chalk. In
those days of support, I learned, remembered, and retained.

I suppose I was fortunate to have sat at the feet of such
masters. But even the worst actor can teach you something,
even if it's something not to do: how not to time, how not to
inflect, how not to move. There is always something to learn.

I suppose it was because of my complete involvement in the
theatre that I eventually became an actor manager. I've always
been determined to try everything. I had dabbled before the St
James's, but suddenly here was my own theatre. Unlike the Old
Vic, where Ralph, John Burrell and myself formed a triumvirate,

this was my very own. For twelve years I was to be my own
man.

I was not a successful manager by any means, but I think it
could be said that I was a pretty courageous one. I was adventur-
ous rather than cautious, and eventually ended up at the thin
end of the box-office takings. I was probably always too ambitious
and my theatre, even when full, could not cope with this. For
example, when I put on the Cleopatras, we were packed every
night of the run, but the only profit I could make was £40 a
week. You can imagine how long I'd have to run a show to gain
any real capital out of that. So, you see, my success record was
not high; it might have been artistically, but not financially.
Consequently the ordinary money man ('angel') was not prepared to back me without reserve, so I had to plunge more and
more of my own cash into it. By the time my twelve years were
up, and they were about to do permanent desecration to my
beautiful St James's, I had spent all my savings in trying to keep
it alive: £60,000 in all – the money I'd made and saved in
Hollywood. At least the only pockets that were hurt were my
own, so I had to pick myself up and get on with life, and go out
and make my daily bread. And that's what I did. It hurt to lose
my theatre, it hurt very much, but there was nothing I could do
about it. The roof had been shifted by the bombing in 1940, it
was an old theatre built in 1820 and a fire hazard. It could not
be licensed by the London County Council any longer unless
£250,000 was spent to make it safe. No investors were available.

I successfully stayed away from management until 1963, when
I was appointed the first director of the National Theatre –
though in a way this was a million miles away from the sort of
actor management I had been involved in before. I was the
artistic director, but I had a board to answer to; I couldn't just
go out on a limb and do as I wished. But I cover most of this in
Confessions of an Actor. In spite of the disagreements over
policies in those years, I would like to think that all of us had
one thing in common: the continuation of the theatre as a fine
art.

I was proud of my position as the director of the National,
and always will be. And I'm certain that the work we did there

was a great credit to the British theatre as a whole. I am convinced that, pound for pound, for a while we were the best troupe of players in the world. They were a sensational company, and they were a company in the true sense of the word. Any one of my team, at any time, could have taken the helm and steered a play into safe harbour. A wonderful company from the second assistant stage manager to the top. I felt I knew them all individually, and I think I did. I might have been the father figure, but I wasn't so in the Victorian sense of the word: my company *did* speak and *were* heard. The proof of my boasting is to look at some of the unknown names of my company then, and how many are known now. I think you'll find that quite a percentage are now in lights above the West End bills in their own right. I hope we all learned something from each other; I'm sure we did. I was able to pass on to them what had been passed on to me. For, although I maintain we must for ever be looking forward, it is still very important to hold on to our theatrical roots and listen.

Out of seventy-nine productions at the National, I only acted in seven and only directed seven, so as to create chances for other younger directors. I never seized the reins and drove the horse myself. We had wonderfully versatile actors; enough people to cast an entirely Scottish play or an Irish one, and what other company could do that? We discovered new plays: the complete spectrum of modern writers from the political Right to the Left. The whole operation, especially casting, fascinated me: moving actors from one part to another, constantly polishing them, constantly letting them emerge in a new form that would stretch them and make them absolutely first class. When I was directing, I always encouraged them to invent like mad, and then it was up to me to see that they didn't foul up the rest of the production. They were great years.

I will never forget that it was Guthrie's remarks to me that changed my gear as an actor. It didn't spew out of my own heart; it was sold to me by the one man from whom I never expected sage advice. Stage directions and practicalities, yes, but never soul matters. I was staggered, and my opinion of him grew enormously, as did my acting.

Acting is the art and craft of presenting a personality to an audience. There are said to be two kinds of actors: straight and character. But everybody who is respected in the profession thinks of himself as a versatile performer. The use of hands, the use of feet, the use of face; but, above all, the acknowledgement of life.

I have always been fascinated by surgeons. Theirs is also a dramatic art. The theatricality of the surgeon in the heat of the operating theatre fighting for the life of a patient under the winged shadow of death is drama at its height.

I have been through a series of illnesses during the past few years and have had to venture under the surgeon's knife myself. The more I discover about my body, in sickness or in health, the more fascinated I become.

I had a friend who was a fine surgeon and I begged him for some time to let me attend one of his operations. He took much persuading, because he thought that, for all my intrigue and bravado, the moment I saw the knife slice into the flesh and blood gush out I would slide to the floor and need to be revived myself.

After some time, however, I was able to convince him that my legs were more stable than a seasick sailor's and he allowed me into *his* theatre. Again came the statement: 'You're in *my* theatre now: if you decide to meet the floor before your good-night mattress, we'll just have to leave you there. We've no time to look after the disarranged stomach of a *well* man.' Fighting, aggressive and understandable words. I was in *his* world now.

'I'm fine,' I said.

'Well if you do pass out, pass *out* and not *in*. If you feel queasy, get out of the way.'

There was a pause. I nodded. He began. There was no chance of me passing out, I was totally absorbed. From the moment the knife went in I was riveted.

I feel that actors should know more about their bodies than perhaps they do. Maybe they should have a copy of Gray's *Anatomy* on their bookshelves along with Shakespeare. I'm not suggesting they should all go and storm the galleries of their local operating theatres, but then again perhaps it wouldn't be a bad idea if they did, to see and be aware of the way the motor works, the blood and the pound of flesh.

After the operation the surgeon realized how intrigued and sincere I was. He knew now that my stomach and head were mine, they did not belong to the nursery floor. I think he was impressed. I certainly was with him. I asked him if I could come again. Later, if anything came up that he thought might interest me, he'd always let me know.

You might think this morbid or macabre, but not at all. I simply wanted to know more about myself. I wanted to get under the make-up, really beneath the skin. I wanted to know every part of me. Every inch, duct and vessel. I'm sure it helped me during my illnesses. I knew exactly what was up, and where it was. I was never frightened, I was just determined to fight. I refused to give in.

When recently I had a kidney removed, I asked quite sincerely if it was possible to be operated on under a local anaesthetic and watch the whole procedure in a mirror. They declined. A pity.

I had always been very athletic, running and lifting weights, using the gym as often as I could. When illness curbed these forms of exercise, I took up swimming and to this day I swim half a mile most mornings. Sixty-six lengths. Monotonous, but worth it. Never give up.

To be fit should be one of an actor's first priorities. Daily exercise is of the utmost importance. The body is an instrument which must be finely tuned and played as often as possible. The actor should be able to control it from the tip of his head to his little toe. He must be able to send messages to any part of it with the speed and skill of a computer. We are living in a machine, a machine of great complexity, and in order to use it properly we must try to understand as much about it as possible. Perhaps part of an actor's course should include a few months of medical studies. Perhaps he should follow the rounds of a houseman in one of the major teaching hospitals, listen in on the lectures and observe. If I was starting today, I know that's what I would do.

Daily exercise is essential when working in front of an audience in the evening, getting tuned up before the performance. The actor should be as fit as a boxer, as poised as a matador, as agile as a ballet dancer. During the course of an evening he may have to work on high voltage for long spells. As Hamlet he must be at top energy level for four hours or more, and then complete the evening with a sword fight. Shakespeare made the actor work for his bread and butter.

As well as the body, the voice must be toned up and, when working, it should be exercised before each performance. This can be difficult if you are sharing a dressing room, but there are always ways round that. Too many actors use the performance itself to warm up, and it shows. It is at least half an hour before everything is running smoothly.

When an actor is not working, it is even more important for him to keep in good shape, though when the horizon is looking on the dark side such self-discipline is hard. It is easier to get under the blankets and hide.

Not only must the body be kept supple and agile, so must the mind. As a writer must write something every day, so should an actor study. And if there is not an immediate part to learn, then he must work on something of his own choice – anything, a speech, a complete role, a poem. Sybil Thorndike always learned a sonnet or some lines of poetry every morning of her life.

All this must sound like blinkered dedication, but I truly believe that in this profession, if you want to reach the heights, this is what you must have. You must be prepared to sacrifice in order to succeed. You must set your goals high and go for them with the pugnacity of a terrier. But remember, to fall into dissipation is easy, for it is a glamorous profession, full of glorious temptations. Place a foot on the first rung and the serpents will appear beckoning with their silky tails, flattering you and begging you to bite the apple.

So many talents, good, raw and rich ones, have been battered against the walls of dissipation and left to drown. The sycophantic serpents are everywhere. Because as a profession it generates glamour, the acolytes queue up to stare at, touch or, if possible, entertain something that they can never be. Their admiration is genuine, but beware, actor, beware. Beware the Greeks.

Above all, do not despair when the hand of criticism plunges into your body and claws at your soul: you must take it, accept it and smile. It is your life and your choice. And beware, look to the opposite. Do not float toward the heavens when the same patronizing person places a hand on the crown of your head and breathes compliments into your vulnerable ear. Everything can change tomorrow. I suppose critics are a grim necessity. There are good ones and bad ones, and ones who simply masquerade as critics but are merely purveyors of columns of gossip, tittle-tattle signifying nothing. Poor creatures who are pushed by their pens and not by their intellects. The good ones are essayists and of immense value to our work. They help, sometimes hinder, but most understand the problems and pitfalls of our profession. Without them some of the great performances of the past would have gone by unrecorded.

Sometimes I think that more critics should be encouraged to sit in on rehearsals so that they could see the amount of work, concentration, belief and love that goes into the construction of a piece, before they take their inky swords to it. But a note of approval for the good critics, the ones who share the same joy that we, the actors, writers and directors have for our world. They're the people whose intellect and pen go hand in hand. They add to our world and very much belong to it, and I imagine it is as painful to them when something doesn't come off as it is to us. I suppose a critic on a daily paper will see more plays in a lifetime than most of us, and many more than once, so it is only natural for him or her to feel he knows more about it than we do. It must be so easy to think of the witty line to ginger up a column, and very tempting to use it, but so unfair on the poor recipient who has had the courage to stand up there and be counted.

I know that, if we are foolish enough to parade ourselves between spotlight and reality, we must be prepared to receive the attention of the pen, but let me plead for thought, care and sincerity, not for mere showmanship.

I have been battered and bruised, praised and lauded. I have laughed and cried, fumed and snorted; I have been beyond the moon and into the depths of despair. But in the end, it has been myself I've had to turn to, believe in and listen to. When the time comes, it is you and only you who knows your truth.

I have concentrated most on my Shakespearean roles in this book because I have found them the most fascinating and their construction still remains clear in my head. I can still see and feel them as though they were happening now. Unlike other parts, the lines have remained with me. They are part of me and I am part of them. The older I get, the more I seem to understand them.

Perhaps I should have spent more time with Shaw, Wilde, Ibsen, Strindberg, Coward, but I'll leave them to the next generation to make their mark upon. Once I saw myself as merely

> . . . *a poor player*
> *That struts and frets his hour upon the stage,*
> *And then is heard no more . . .*

But now I know we can remain. We now have film, television, tape. We can stay hereafter to be referred to, looked up and criticized, laughed at or admired, a hundred years from now. But much as I love these media – indeed I must owe at least a third of my acting life to them – they cannot truly show what it is like to have been there. Once printed, they will never change, that moment is there forever. There will never be the smell or the adrenalin on celluloid. The real moment will have gone.

Film is the director's medium, television the writer's, but the theatre is the actor's. When the actor is on stage, it is he and he alone who drives the moment. The audience have no choice but to remain in his faith or leave. That's the true excitement, the real magic of the profession. The actor on stage is all-powerful, for once the curtain rises he is in control. There is nothing the director or author can do once the house lights dim and the tabs go up. The actor can choose to do or say anything he likes, he is the governor, he cracks the whip.

It is the author and the director who bite their nails at the back of the stalls between over-indulgent intakes of alcohol, not the actor.

Once the actor begins to motor and the initial nerves are out of the way, his inward smile is Cheshire-like as he flexes and enjoys the muscles of his art.

Breathing in the thick, warm air, feeling the expectancy of the house as it waits for your next moment. Timing a pause for perfection. Feeling the lungs bellow in and out as the voice hits the heights of its power. Never giving too much; always making them want more. Making a gesture and holding it, knowing that all eyes have moved with you. Hearing laughter as it moves through the theatre like a giant wave, aware that it has been caused by you. Knowing that tears are there for the asking. Controlling every eye in the house, making your thoughts theirs. Taking them on the journey with you, lending their ears to your mind. Frightening them, exciting them, loving them, holding them in the palm of your hand, Gulliver and the Lilliputians. Cuddling them, cajoling them, caressing them. Without them you do not exist. Without them you are a man alone in a room with memories and a mirror. Without them you are nothing. An actor without an audience is a painter without a brush. Of course you can always perform in your head, but where's the satisfaction?

As I have already said, it starts at the very beginning by the family fireside, where the child demands attention: 'Look at me, look at me.' Once attention has been gained, it's keeping it that's important. It is then that the talent to amuse, entertain, provoke shines through; you can soon see who are going to be actors and who stage managers. It is then that you can see the future.

Never underestimate the audience, never patronize them, because, if you do, they will know. They are far more intelligent than you may think. They pay your bills and fill your stomach. Without them you are in an empty room again with a bare cupboard. You must always treat them with respect, be they one or a thousand. If the house is small, never give a small performance. Never cheapen yourself or your profession. It is one of the oldest and best. Remember the court jester: he didn't dare perform badly, he was always on the high wire.

I can no longer work in the theatre, but the thrill will never leave me. The lights and the combat. The intimacy between the audience and me during the soliloquies in *Hamlet* and *Richard III* – we were like lovers.

At my age you do things when you think of them, because you don't know when the great axe is going to fall.

I am seventy-eight going on eighteen. I have just filmed a new television series for Granada. I have made a hologram, which means I will appear nightly in a new West End musical in 1986. When the television is over, I am making a pop record . . . and so it goes on.

That's an actor's life: complete freedom and versatility. Everything changes as I have said. But then again, nothing changes. All we need is an old cigar box and somebody to take notice.

EPILOGUE

LETTER TO A YOUNG ACTRESS

On 24 January 1947, I made a speech at the opening of the Old Vic School, which was run by my close friends and colleagues Michel St Denis, Glen Byam Shaw and George Devine. This is part of what I said to the incoming students:

> An actor must above all be a great understander, either by intuition, observation or both, and that puts him on the level with a doctor, a priest or a philosopher. If I can get more from him than just belief, then I feel fortunate and overjoyed . . . There are many dimensions in the art of acting, but NONE of them . . . are good or interesting . . . unless they are invested with the appearance, or complete illusions of truth. The difference between the actual truth and the illusion of the truth is what you are about to learn. You will not finish learning it until you are dead.

Soon to be at the Old Vic School was a young woman who came to be acknowledged as a great actress, and who has for twenty-five years been my pride and joy: my beloved wife Joan Plowright.

I had fallen in love with her Margery Pinchwife in *The Country Wife*, marvelled at her virtuosity as the Old Lady in Ionesco's *The Chairs*, and been quite knocked out by her Beatie Bryant in Arnold Wesker's *Roots*. Then she came to play Jean Rice with me in *The Entertainer*. Later she went back to George Devine at the Court to play the title role in Shaw's *Major Barbara*. It was then that I wrote to a young actress.

Dear Joan,

I do hope you won't mind, pet, a few words of encouragement, and a few of criticism, as you said you wouldn't last night when I was in a mad rush after your (very late I must say) show, from your old Dad.

First of all I was really very impressed by how far you had managed to go to collar this not at all rewarding part along most difficult new lines for you.

By the way, please tell Georgie, who came to talk about *All's Well That Ends Well*, that I am *absolutely* happy, having seen you in this, that it will hold no terrors for you. You could knock off Helena on your dainty black head, darling. You have an absolute natural poetic quality and without any sign of strain, which is the whole bloody thing.

Now then. I think when you essay to alter your personality as radically as you are required to do for Barbara you must be prepared to throw out some of those qualities which have stood you in good stead in your earlier triumphs at this theatre.

You have an absolutely marvellous uncalculated, impish sense of humour which is strongly laced with an aptitude for self-mockery. This last can be an invaluable but also a dangerous quality which should be used judiciously . . . the first is priceless, but must not always be relied upon because it will not *always* get you out of a hole.

In any untoward circumstance which might make one unusually self-conscious, or when overtired, the basic elements of our personality will predominate. Naturally, as they are the first things within us, we unconsciously grab hold of them to make us think we can do it at all, as any mannerism is developed subconsciously to cover up some weakness . . . disjointed pauses by one who is frightened of drying up . . . exaggerated gait in one who thinks he is ungainly, e.g. J.G., etc.

But in this role, or any in which the background is different from our own, we must be strong and prepared to face the fact that these elements may not be suitable and bloody well create something else that is.

Here we were last night, finding ourselves prepared for the canopied presence of a South Kensington family, *one* member of which is a bit different. How? *Not* by a basic difference of natural type (although I suppose you could claim she took after Father) but by a basic difference of spiritual identification. In this case, the impish humour and self-mockery tends, in these circumstances, to say to the audience, 'Just look at me, the rebel of the Royal Court, hobnobbing with all these stiff and starchy folk.'

And that puts you at a disadvantage and takes away from your success in showing the *real* difference between Barbara and the society to which she belongs.

There is one word which describes what you should bring on to the stage with you in this part. RADIANCE. And don't be frightened of it, pet, and don't let self mockery guy you out of it. Self-mockery can have its bellyful on other occasions.

I think I told you how hard it was for me not to be self-conscious in the 'Crispin' speech . . . it was 1937 and we were all a highly debunking generation.

You are a wonderfully gifted and beautifully disciplined actress . . . do not be shy of Dedication. Grasp hold of it. We can still keep our old sense of humour, but in its *place*; the indiscriminating allowance of it . . . has taken the top off many a brilliant actor. Acting is basically a humourless craft, and that's what makes people like us suffer so.

I think you are a little frightened of the part and it's hard to love anything you're frightened of. But you *must* love Barbara. Love her as she's never been loved before. Love is (among other things) the exaltation of understanding. Now *understanding* is the absolute *must* in our work, and the means whereby we can *inform*. Love is the means whereby we can bring that information home.

We must love Iago or Caliban, we must even love the unrewarding Jean Rice! Ours not to reason why, ours to apprehend and impart. We must never shirk the preparation in the wings, the practising of the old self-hypnotic act to transform ourselves completely before we step on to the stage.

Please don't think I am saying it is a bad thing to be frightened of a part at the beginning.

A humble approach to our work is essential and there is a dreadfully stern law which ordains that 'No True Artist May Expect Satisfaction From His Work.' But how do we equate the essential humility towards the work with the full possession of the confidence required to carry it off?

Not that last night's audience were given any other impression than that you were sailing along confident in your prowess and presenting a perfectly *plausible* Barbara for their enjoyment and approval. But you and I know that you have brought her towards yourself . . . and *into you* . . . instead of going out to her. And that is what leaves you with that niggling sense of dissatisfaction.

One or two things. Your back is straight and beautiful (Christ, those corsets in this weather) but don't be too far back on your heels. Keep your knees flexible and swing a *tiny* little more on the walk. Your hands are exquisite and you can afford yourself a little more consciousness of this. If you scratch your nose, see that it is a charming gesture (I mean in this sort of thing)!

Your voice gets better all the time and can be rich and lovely when you want it to . . . keep it clear and don't let emotion make it plummy. It is one of the hardest things to do in our work . . . to plumb emotion to its very depths and still allow the audience to hear every single f . . . . . g word. You don't know how lucky you are to be able to cry at will on stage . . . Johnny G never stops . . . and as I've told you I've never been able to do it in my life. But I've been able to make people believe that I can . . . and that is what it's all about, isn't it?

I hope this has been of some use to you, my darling, I'd love to help any time I can . . . but only if you feel the need of it. You go your own sweet way and sweet may it be at all times. I know it will always be sweet to your devoted

Larry

PERFORMANCES

THEATRE

1907   Born on 22 May

1917   *Julius Caesar* (Shakespeare), role: Brutus, dir. Geoffrey Heald, All Saints School

       Twelfth Night (Shakespeare), role: Maria, dir, Geoffrey Heald, All Saints School

1920   *The Taming of the Shrew* (Shakespeare), role: Katharina,
1922   dir. Geoffrey Heald, All Saints School and Memorial Theatre, Stratford-upon-Avon

1923   *A Midsummer Night's Dream* (Shakespeare), role: Puck, dir. W. H. A. Cowell, St Edward's School, Oxford

1924   *Macbeth* (Shakespeare), role: Lennox, dir. Beatrice Wilson, Central School of Speech Training and Dramatic Art (CSSTDA), St Christopher, Letchworth

       Byron (Law), role: Suliot Officer, dir. Henry Oscar, CSSTDA, Century, London

1925   *Henry IV, Part II* (Shakespeare), roles: Thomas of Clarence and Snare, dir. L. E. Berman, CSSTDA, Regent Theatre, London

       Unfailing Instinct (Frank), role: Armand St Cyr, dir. Julian Frank, CSSTDA, Hippodrome, Brighton, and UK tour

       The Ghost Train (Ridley), role: Policeman, dir. Julian Frank, CSSTDA, Hippodrome, Brighton, and UK tour

1925–6   Member of Lena Ashwell Players

       The Tempest (Shakespeare), role: Antonio, dir. Lena Ashwell, Century Theatre, London

       Julius Caesar (Shakespeare), role: Flavius, dir. Lena Ashwell, Century Theatre, London

       Henry VIII (Shakespeare), role: First Serving Man, dir. Lewis Casson, Empire Theatre, London

The Cenci (Shelley), role: Servant to Orsino, dir. Lewis
    Casson, Empire Theatre, London

1926   *The Marvellous History of St Bernard* (Ghéon), role: Min-
    strel, dir. A. E. Filmer, Kingsway Theatre, London

The Barber and the Cow (Davies), small part, dir. H.K.
    Ayliff, UK tour

The Farmer's Wife (Phillpotts), role: Richard Croaker, dir.
    H. K. Ayliff, UK tour

1926–7   Member of Birmingham Repertory Theatre Company

1927   *Something to Talk About* (Phillpotts), role: Guy Sydney,
    dir. W. G. Fay, Birmingham Repertory Theatre

The Well of the Saints (Synge), role: Mat Simon, dir. W.
    G. Fay, Birmingham Repertory Theatre

The Third Finger (Whittaker), role: Tom Hardcastle, dir.
    W. G. Fay, Birmingham Repertory Theatre

The Mannoch Family (McClymond), role: Peter Mannoch,
    dir. W. G. Fay, Birmingham Repertory Theatre

The Comedian (Ghéon), role: walk on, dir. W. G. Fay,
    Birmingham Repertory Theatre

Uncle Vanya (Chekhov), role: Vanya, dir. W. G fay, Bir-
    mingham Repertory Theatre

All's Well That Ends Well (Shakespeare), role: Parolles,
    dir. W. G. Fay, Birmingham Repertory Theatre

The Pleasure Garden (Mayor), role: Young man, dir. W.
    G. Fay, Birmingham Repertory Theatre

She Stoops to Conquer (Goldsmith), role: Tony Lumpkin,
    dir. W. G. Fay, Birmingham Repertory Theatre

Quality Street (Barrie), role: Ensign Blades, dir. W. G.
    Fay, Birmingham Repertory Theatre

Bird in Hand (Drinkwater), role: Gerald Arnwood, dir.
    John Drinkwater, Birmingham Repertory Theatre

Advertising April (Farjeon and Horsnell), role: Mervyn
    Jones, dir. W. G. Fay, Birmingham Repertory Theatre

The Silver Box (Galsworthy), role: Jack Barthwick, dir. W.
    G. Fay, Birmingham Repertory Theatre

The Adding Machine (Rice), role: Young Man, dir. W. G.
    Fay, Birmingham Repertory Theatre

Aren't Women Wonderful? (Dean), role: Ben Hawley, dir.
    W. G. Fay, Birmingham Repertory Theatre

The Road to Ruin (Holcroft), role: Mr Milford, dir. W. G.
    Fay, Birmingham Repertory Theatre

1928   *The Adding Machine* (Rice), role: Young Man, dir. W. G. Fay, Court Theatre, London

Macbeth (Shakespeare), role: Malcolm, dir. H. K. Ayliff, Court Theatre, London

Back to Methuselah (Shaw), role: Martellus, dir. H. K. Ayliff, Court Theatre, London

Harold (Tennyson), role: Harold, dir. H. K. Ayliff, Court Theatre, London

The Taming of the Shrew (Shakespeare), role: A Lord, dir. H. K. Ayliff, Court Theatre, London

Bird in Hand (Drinkwater), role: Gerald Arnwood, dir. John Drinkwater, Royalty Theatre, London

The Dark Path (John), role: Graham Birley, dir. Evan John, Royalty Theatre, London

Journey's End (Sherriff), role: Captain Stanhope, dir. James Whale, Apollo Theatre, London

1929   *Beau Geste* (Dean and Mann), role: Beau, dir. Basil Dean, His Majesty's Theatre, London

The Circle of Chalk (Klabund and Laver), role: Prince Po, New Theatre, London

Paris Bound (Barry), role: Richard Parish, dir. Arthur Hopkins, Lyric Theatre, London

The Stranger Within (Wilbur), role: John Hardy, dir. Reginald Bach, Garrick Theatre, London

Murder on the Second Floor (Vosper), role: Hugh Bromilow, dir. William Mollison, Eltinge Theatre, New York

The Last Enemy (Harvey), role: Jerry Warrender, dir. Tom Walls, Fortune Theatre, London

1930   *After All* (van Druten), role: Ralph, dir. Auriol Lee, Arts Theatre, London

Private Lives (Coward), role: Victor Prynne, dir. Noël Coward, Phoenix Theatre, London

1931   *Private Lives* (Coward), role: Victor Prynne, dir. Noël Coward, Times Square Theatre, New York

1933   *The Rats of Norway* (Winter), role: Steven Beringer, dir. Raymond Massey, Playhouse Theatre, London

The Green Bay Tree (Shairp), role: Julian Dulcimer, dir. Jed Harris, Cort Theatre, New York

1934   *Biography* (Behrman), role: Richard Kurt, dir. Noël Coward, Globe Theatre, London

Queen of Scots (Daviot), role: Bothwell, dir. John Gielgud, New Theatre, London

Theatre Royal (Ferber and Kaufman), role: Anthony Cavendish, dir. Noël Coward, Lyric Theatre, London

1935   *Ringmaster* (Winter), role: Peter Hammond, dir. Raymond Massey, Shaftesbury Theatre, London

Golden Arrow (Thompson and Cunard), role: Richard Harben, dir. Laurence Olivier, Whitehall Theatre, London

Romeo and Juliet (Shakespeare), roles: Romeo, then Mercutio, dir. John Gielgud, New Theatre, London

1936   *Bees on the Boatdeck* (Priestley), role: Robert Patch, dir. Laurence Olivier and Ralph Richardson, Lyric Theatre, London

1937–49   Member of Old Vic Company

1937   *Hamlet* (Shakespeare), role: Hamlet, dir. Tyrone Guthrie, Old Vic Theatre, London

Twelfth Night (Shakespeare), role: Sir Toby Belch, dir. Tyrone Guthrie, Old Vic Theatre, London

Henry V (Shakespeare), role: Henry, dir. Tyrone Guthrie, Old Vic Theatre

Hamlet (Shakespeare), role: Hamlet, dir. Tyrone Guthrie, Elsinore, Denmark

Macbeth (Shakespeare), role: Macbeth, dir. Michel St Denis, Old Vic Theatre and New Theatre, London

1938   *Othello* (Shakespeare), role: Iago, dir. Tyrone Guthrie, Old Vic Theatre, London

The King of Nowhere (Bridie), role: Vivaldi, dir. Tyrone Guthrie, Old Vic Theatre, London

Coriolanus (Shakespeare), role: Coriolanus, dir. Lewis Casson, Old Vic Theatre, London

1939   *No Time for Comedy* (Behrman), role: Gaylord Easterbrook, dir. Guthrie McClintic, Ethel Barrymore Theatre, New York

1940   *Romeo and Juliet* (Shakespeare), role: Romeo, dir. Laurence Olivier, 51st Street Theatre, New York

1944–5   *Peer Gynt* (Ibsen), role: Button Moulder, dir. Tyrone Guthrie and Robert Helpmann, New Theatre, London, and Paris and New York

Arms and the Man (Shaw), role: Sergius Saranoff, dir. John Burrell, New Theatre, London, and Paris and New York

Richard III (Shakespeare), role: Gloucester, dir. John Burrell, New Theatre, London, and Paris and New York

1945–6 *Uncle Vanya* (Chekhov), role: Astrov, dir. John Burrell, New Theatre, London

Henry IV, Part I (Shakespeare), role: Hotspur, dir. John Burrell, New Theatre, London

Henry IV, Part II (Shakespeare), role: Justice Shallow, dir. John Burrell, New Theatre, London

Oedipus Rex (Sophocles), role: Oedipus, dir. Michel St Denis, New Theatre, London

The Critic (Sheridan), role: Mr Puff, dir. Miles Malleson, New Theatre, London

1946 *King Lear* (Shakespeare), role: Lear, dir. Laurence Olivier, New Theatre, London

1948 *The School for Scandal* (Sheridan), role: Sir Peter Teazle, dir. Laurence Olivier, tour of New Zealand and Australia

Richard III (Shakespeare), role: Gloucester, dir. John Burrell, tour of New Zealand and Australia

The Skin of Our Teeth (Wilder), role: Mr Antrobus, dir. Laurence Olivier, tour of New Zealand and Australia

1949 *Richard III* (Shakespeare), role: Gloucester, dir. John Burrell, New Theatre, London

The School for Scandal (Sheridan), role: Sir Peter Teazle, dir. Laurence Olivier, New Theatre, London

Antigone (Anouilh), role: Chorus, dir. Laurence Olivier, New Theatre, London

1950 *Venus Observed* (Fry), role: Duke of Altair, dir. Laurence Olivier, St James's Theatre, London

1951 *Caesar and Cleopatra* (Shaw), role: Caesar, dir. Michael Benthall, St James's Theatre, London, and Ziegfeld Theatre, New York

Antony and Cleopatra (Shakespeare), role: Antony, dir. Michael Benthall, St James's Theatre, London, and Ziegfeld Theatre, New York

1953 *The Sleeping Prince* (Rattigan), role: Grand Duke, dir. Laurence Olivier, Phoenix Theatre, London

1955 *Twelfth Night* (Shakespeare), role: Malvolio, dir. John Gielgud, Memorial Theatre, Stratford-upon-Avon

Macbeth (Shakespeare), role: Macbeth, dir. Glen Byam Shaw, Memorial Theatre, Stratford-upon-Avon

Titus Andronicus (Shakespeare), role: Titus, dir. Peter Brook, Memorial Theatre, Stratford-upon-Avon

1957   *The Entertainer* (Osborne), role: Archie Rice, dir. Tony Richardson, Royal Court Theatre, London

Titus Andronicus (Shakespeare), role: Titus, dir. Peter Brook, Memorial Theatre Co. European tour and Stoll Theatre, London

1957–8   *The Entertainer* (Osborne), role: Archie Rice, dir. Tony Richardson, Palace Theatre, London, and Royale Theatre, New York

1959   *Coriolanus* (Shakespeare), role: Coriolanus, dir. Peter Hall, Memorial Theatre, Stratford-upon-Avon

1960   *Rhinoceros* (Ionesco), role: Berenger, dir. Orson Welles, Royal Court and Strand Theatres, London

1960–61   *Becket* (Anouilh), role. Becket, dir. Peter Glenville, St James's Theatre and Hudson Theatre, New York

1962   *The Broken Heart* (Ford), roles: Prologue and Bassanes, dir. Laurence Olivier, Chichester Festival Theatre, Chichester

Uncle Vanya (Chekhov), role: Astrov, dir. Laurence Olivier, Chichester Festival Theatre, Chichester

1962–73   Director of the National Theatre Company

1962   *Semi-Detached* (Turner), role: Fred Midway, dir. Tony Richardson, Saville Theatre, London

1963   *Uncle Vanya* (Chekhov), role: Astrov, dir. Laurence Olivier, Chichester Festival Theatre, Chichester, and Old Vic Theatre, London

The Recruiting Officer (Farquhar), role: Captain Brazen, dir. William Gaskill, Old Vic Theatre, London

1964   *Othello* (Shakespeare), role: Othello, dir. John Dexter, Chichester Festival Theatre, Chichester, and Old Vic Theatre, London

The Master Builder (Ibsen), role: Halvard Solness, dir. Peter Wood, Old Vic Theatre, London

1965   *Othello* (Shakespeare), role: Othello, dir. John Dexter, Moscow and Berlin

Love for Love (Congreve), role: Tattle, dir. Peter Wood, Old Vic Theatre, London, and Moscow and Berlin

1967   *The Dance of Death* (Strindberg), role: Edgar, dir. Glen Byam Shaw, Old Vic Theatre, London, and tour of Canada

Love for Love (Congreve), role: Tattle, dir. Peter Wood, tour of Canada

A Flea in her Ear (Feydeau), role: Plucheux, dir. Jacques Charon, tour of Canada

1969   *Home and Beauty* (Maugham), role: A. B. Raham, dir. Frank Dunlop, Old Vic Theatre, London

Three Sisters (Chekhov), role: Chebutikin, dir. Laurence Olivier, Old Vic Theatre, London, and Los Angeles

1970   *The Merchant of Venice* (Shakespeare), role: Shylock, dir. Jonathan Miller, Old Vic Theatre, London

1971   *Long Day's Journey Into Night* (O'Neill), role: James Tyrone, dir. Michael Blakemore, Old Vic Theatre and New Theatre, London

1973   *Saturday, Sunday, Monday* (de Filippo), role: Antonio, dir. Franco Zeffirelli, Old Vic Theatre, London

The Party (Griffiths), role: John Tagg, dir. John Dexter, Old Vic Theatre, London

FILMS

Including films made for television. The year is the release date. American film titles are given in brackets.

1930   *The Temporary Widow*, dir. Gustav Ucicky

Too Many Crooks, dir. George King

1931   *Potiphar's Wife (Her Strange Desire)*, dir. Maurice Elvery

Friends and Lovers, dir. Victor Schertzinger

The Yellow Passport (The Yellow Ticket), dir. Raoul Walsh

1932   *Westward Passage*, dir. Robert Milton

1933   *Perfect Understanding*, dir. Cyril Gardner

No Funny Business (The Professional Co-respondents), dir. John Stafford and Victor Hanbury

1935   *Moscow Nights (I Stand Condemned)*, dir. Anthony Asquith

1936   *As You Like It*, dir. Paul Czinner

Conquest of the Air, dir. A. Shaw, J. M. Saunders, A. Esway and Z. Korda

1937   *Fire Over England*, dir. William K. Howard

Twenty-One Days, dir. Basil Dean

1938   *The Divorce of Lady X*, dir. Tim Whelan

1939   *Q Planes (Clouds Over Europe)*, dir. Tim Whelan

Wuthering Heights, dir. William Wyler

1940   *Rebecca*, dir. Alfred Hitchcock

Pride and Pre judice, dir. Robert Z. Leonard

1941   *Words for Battle,* commentary only, dir. Humphrey Jennings

Lady Hamilton (That Hamilton Woman), dir. Alexander Korda

49th Parallel, dir. Michael Powell

1943   *The Demi-Paradise,* dir. Anthony Asquith

1945   *Henry V,* dir. Laurence Olivier

1948   *Hamlet,* dir. Laurence Olivier

1951   *The Magic Box,* dir. Laurence Olivier

1952   *Carrie,* dir. William Wyler

1953   *A Queen is Crowned,* voice only, prod. Castleton Knight

The Beggar's Opera, dir. Peter Brook

1955   *Richard III,* dir. Laurence Olivier

1957   *The Prince and the Showgirl,* dir. Laurence Olivier

1959   *The Devil's Disciple,* dir. Guy Hamilton

1960   *Spartacus,* dir. Stanley Kubrick

The Entertainer, dir. Tony Richardson

1961   *The Power and the Glory,* dir. Marc Daniels

1962   *Term of Trial,* dir. Peter Glenville

1963   *Uncle Vanya,* dir. Laurence Olivier

1965   *Bunny Lake is Missing,* dir. Otto Preminger

Othello, dir. Stuart Burge

1966   *Khartoum,* dir. Basil Dearden

1968   *Romeo and Juliet,* voice only, dir. Franco Zeffirelli

The Shoes of the Fisherman, dir. Michael Anderson

1969   *Oh! What A Lovely War,* dir. Richard Attenborough

The Battle of Britain, dir. Guy Hamilton

The Dance of Death, dir. David Giles

David Copperfield, dir. Delbert Mann

1970   *Three Sisters,* dir. Laurence Olivier

1971   *Nicholas and Alexandra,* dir. Franklin J. Schaffner

1972   *Lady Caroline Lamb,* dir. Robert Bolt

Sleuth, dir. Joseph L. Mankiewicz

1975   *Love Among the Ruins,* dir. George Cukor

1976   *The Seven Per Cent Solution,* dir. Herbert Ross

Marathon Man, dir. John Schlesinger

1977   *Jesus of Nazareth,* dir. Franco Zeffirelli

A Bridge Too Far, dir. Richard Attenborough

1978   *The Betsy,* dir. Daniel Petrie

The Boys from Brazil, dir. Franklin J. Schaffner

1979   *A Little Romance*, dir. George Roy Hill
           Dracula, dir. John Badham
1980   *The Jazz Singer*, dir. Richard Fleischer
           Made *Inchon* (unreleased), dir. Terence Young
1981   *Clash of the Titans*, dir. Desmond David
1984   *The Bounty*, dir. Roger Donaldson
           The Last Days of Pompeii, dir. Peter Hunt
1985   *Wagner*, dir. Tony Palmer
           The Jigsaw Man, dir. Terence Young
           Wild Geese II, dir. Peter Hunt

TELEVISION

1937   *Macbeth* (Shakespeare), excerpts, role: Macbeth, BBC
1958   *John Gabriel Borkman* (Ibsen), role: Borkman, ATV
1959   *The Moon and Sixpence* (Maugham), role: Charles Strickland, NBC
1967   *Theatre Royal*, charity perf., role: Prologue (Day Lewis), Rediffusion
1969   *Male of the Species* (Owen), role: host/narrator, NBC
1972   *Long Day's Journey Into Night* (O'Neill), role: James Tyrone, ATV
1973   *The Merchant of Venice* (Shakespeare), role: Shylock, ATV
1974   *World at War*, role: narrator, Thames
1976   *The Collection* (Pinter), role: Harry Kane, Granada
           Cat on a Hot Tin Roof (Williams), role: Big Daddy, Granada
1978   *Come Back, Little Sheba* (Inge), role: Doc Delaney, Granada
           Daphne Laureola (Bridie), role: Sir Joseph Pitts, Granada
           Saturday, Sunday, Monday (de Filippo), role: Antonio, Granada
1981   *Brideshead Revisited* (Waugh), role: Lord Marchmain, Granada
1982   *A Voyage Round My Father* (Mortimer), role: Clifford Mortimer, Thames
1983   *King Lear* (Shakespeare), role: Lear, Granada
           A Talent for Murder (Choderov and Panama), role: Dr Wainwright, BBC

1984   *Mr Halpern and Mr Johnson* (Goldstein), role: Mr Halpern, HTV

The Ebony Tower (Fowles), role: Henry Breasley, Granada

1986   *Lost Empires* (Priestley), role: Harry Burrard, Granada

INDEX

INDEX

TOM GALLACHER

JOURNEYMAN

'For reasons I'm ashamed of now, I was living in Montreal in the spring of 1967.'

Bill Thompson is hiding out in scruffy digs on the city's lower east side, a refugee from his own father and his father's ambitions for him. He meets Glaswegian Hugh Gillespie. From completely different backgrounds, yet they grow close. Hugh, pursuer rather than pursued, is seeking out a long vanished childhood friend.

Both sense that their lives are at a turning point. Against the blare and glare of Montreal's Expo 67 – the World Fair – optimism, idealism and wishful thinking are shown up and reduced down in the harsh light of reality.

'A perfect command of dialogue and of pace'
Norman Shrapnel in The Guardian

'A fast-paced novel with some of the elements of a thriller . . . It is an excellent read'
British Book News

LAURENCE OLIVIER

CONFESSIONS OF AN ACTOR

Laurence Olivier has become a legend in his own lifetime. No
classical actor has been such a dazzling star. No star has been
such a magnificent actor.

In this marvellous autobiography Laurence Olivier at last tells
his own story: his brilliant career as actor, director, film-maker
and producer; his role as husband to three women, including
the beautiful, wayward but doomed Vivien Leigh; and his many
friendships – with Sir Ralph Richardson, Noël Coward and Sir
Winston Churchill, to name but a few.

CONFESSIONS OF AN ACTOR is more than just a memoir, it
is a deeply felt testament by one of the most astonishingly
gifted artists of all time.

'A remarkable book'

Daily Telegraph

'Those who seek an account of the splendours and miseries of
an actor's life will be richly rewarded'

The New York Times Book Review

J. M. O'NEILL

OPEN CUT

Hennessy lived in London: grafted, struggled and eked out his days in a London respectable people are careful never to see. A construction-site world of 'kerbside sweat, open-cut trenches, timbered shafts'. A bleak, desolate world of whisky-dulled pain, casual brutality and corruption.

But Hennessy planned a change to his station in life. An abrupt and violent change.

'O'Neill's prose, like the winter wind, is cutting and sharp'
British Book News

'Fascinating'

Yorkshire Post

THOMAS KENEALLY

VICTIM OF THE AURORA

In the waning years of the Edwardian era, a group of gentle-men adventurers wait out a raging blizzard in the perpetual darkness of the Antarctic winter, poised for a strike at the South Pole. As the storm lifts, a new challenge faces Captain Eugene Stewart – to discover which of his twenty-five care-fully chosen men has become a murderer. The quest for adventure has become a quest for justice.

'I was riveted by this tale of a man fighting the elements and his fellow explorers'

Daily Telegraph

'The absolute dark, absolute cold of the Antarctic is skilfully evoked'

The Sunday Times

'A powerful and subtle writer . . . a remarkable novel'

Spectator

Current and forthcoming titles from Sceptre

LAURENCE OLIVIER

CONFESSIONS OF AN ACTOR

TOM GALLACHER

JOURNEYMAN

J. M. O'NEILL

OPEN CUT

THOMAS KENEALLY

VICTIM OF THE AURORA

ANATOLY MARCHENKO

MY TESTIMONY

BOOKS OF DISTINCTION